150 BAKING recipes 	*150* recipes 	*150* recipes 	**150 & MUFFIN** recipes 
150 FAST & SIMPLE recipes 	**150 GRANDMA'S** recipes 	**150 HEALTHY** recipes 	**150 INDIAN** recipes
150 ONE-POT recipes 	**150 PASTA** recipes 	**150 SLOW COOKER** recipes 	**150 STIR-FRY** recipes 
	150 STUDENT recipes 	**150 TAPAS** recipes 	**150 VEGETARIAN** recipes 

150

ONE-POT
recipes

....

INSPIRED IDEAS FOR
EVERYDAY COOKING

CONTENTS

INTRODUCTION	4
POULTRY	6
MEAT	56
FISH & SEAFOOD	106
VEGETABLES	156
BEANS	206
INDEX	254

INTRODUCTION

Maximum flavour for minimum effort, that's the real deal with these magnificent one-pot meals! One-pot cooking creates mouthwatering meals that have been created in a single pot. The vast majority of the recipes that follow are prepared using a single pot, which might be a saucepan, frying pan, casserole dish, wok or roasting tin, so that everything is cooked together in the same pot on the hob or in the oven, allowing time for the ingredients to meld together and create a meal with optimum flavour and appeal. There are just a few recipes where an extra frying pan is required but these are designed to add extra flavour to the final dish.

Take inspiration from this fantastic collection of delicious one-pot wonders, including hearty, slow-cooked stews and casseroles, warming soups, quick-cook stir-fries and tempting roasts and bakes, all providing no-fuss meals to please everyone.

Some can be made ahead, others can be left to simmer away while you get on with other things, making them ideal for satisfying family meals or entertaining the easy way. Some one-pot recipes provide tasty budget-friendly meals too, making them the perfect pots of goodness for frugal family fare.

Keep accompaniments simple and serve one pots with boiled new potatoes, baked potatoes, creamy mash, cooked rice or couscous, garlic bread, flatbreads or just plenty of crusty bread to mop up the delicious juices.

If you want to feed the family, cater for a crowd or simply catch up with a few friends for a casual midweek meal, you'll find something to suit everyone and every occasion in this comprehensive collection of stress-free and satisfying one-pot meals. After all, a bubbling pot of flavour-packed comfort food, coupled with some enticing aromas wafting from the kitchen, is sure to win over your guests and tempt them to the table!

First on the menu is an appealing selection of popular poultry one-pot meals. Our top poultry picks include soul-warming soups like Chicken

Noodle Soup or Cream of Chicken Soup, as well as sustaining stews such as Turkey & Barley Stew, Hunter's Chicken and Spiced Chicken Stew. If casual entertaining is the order of the day, then opt for one of our spruced-up poultry one-pots like Duck Legs with Olives, Coq au Vin or Moroccan-style Turkey.

Next up is a collection of marvellous meaty mouthfuls, including some rustic one pots like One-Pot Lasagne, Pork Hot Pot and Sausage & Bean Casserole. Bold flavours come to the fore in our selection of rich and hearty casseroles such as ever-popular Hearty Beef Stew, Chilli Con Carne or Cinnamon Lamb Casserole. Homely favourites include Ham & Lentil Soup and Beef in Beer with Herb Dumplings, and you don't need a traditional clay pot to create our delicious and meltingly tender Tagine of Lamb.

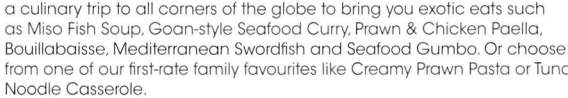

Our next chapter focuses on fabulous fish and seafood one pots and we take a culinary trip to all corners of the globe to bring you exotic eats such as Miso Fish Soup, Goan-style Seafood Curry, Prawn & Chicken Paella, Bouillabaisse, Mediterranean Swordfish and Seafood Gumbo. Or choose from one of our first-rate family favourites like Creamy Prawn Pasta or Tuna Noodle Casserole.

For some super vegetable-based one-pot meals featuring on-trend grains, choose from stand-out dishes like Mexican Quinoa Chilli or Squash, Kale & Farro Stew, or take your pick from no-fuss one pots such as Potato & Mushroom Pie or Persian Herb Frittata. If you want to boost your daily vegetable intake, try tempting dishes like Spanish Vegetable Stew, Cabbage & Walnut Stir-fry or Onion & Root Vegetable Winter Roast.

Finally, we feature some truly warming one pots showcasing a range of wholesome beans and pulses. Classic comfort food to keep the chills at bay includes Tuscan Bean Stew, Ribollita and Vegetable & Lentil Casserole, or for those who fancy something a bit spicier, Sweet Potato & Chickpea Curry or Chilli Bean Stew are sure to hit the spot.

INTRODUCTION

POULTRY

ROASTED DUCK SOUP WITH MUSHROOMS & EGGS	8
ROAST CHICKEN WINGS WITH GARLIC	10
CHICKEN NOODLE SOUP	12
TURKEY & LENTIL SOUP	14
DUCK LEGS WITH OLIVES	16
CHICKEN SOUP WITH LEEKS & RICE	18
CHICKEN & LENTIL SOUP	19
SAFFRON CHICKEN & VEGETABLE STEW	20
CHICKEN WITH 40 GARLIC CLOVES	22
BAKED CHICKEN & CHORIZO PAELLA	24
CREAM OF CHICKEN SOUP	26
TURKEY & BARLEY STEW	28
CHICKEN CACCIATORE	29
STIR-FRIED TURKEY WITH CRANBERRY GLAZE	30
CHICKEN WITH GOAT'S CHEESE & MUSHROOM SAUCE	31
CHICKEN & SWEET POTATO BAKE	32
CHICKEN & APPLE POT	34
CHICKEN & PUMPKIN CASSEROLE	36
TURKEY STROGANOFF	38
ITALIAN TURKEY STEW	40
DUCK JAMBALAYA STEW	42
MEXICAN CHLCKEN, CHILLI & POTATO POT	44
HUNTER'S CHICKEN	46
COQ AU VIN	47
SPICED CHICKEN STEW	48
CHICKEN & BARLEY STEW	50
ROAST CHICKEN	52
MOROCCAN-STYLE TURKEY	54

ROASTED DUCK SOUP WITH MUSHROOMS & EGGS

Serves: 4 **Prep: 10 mins, plus soaking** **Cook: 50 mins**

Ingredients

- 15 g/½ oz dried shiitake mushrooms
- 1.7 litres/3 pints chicken or duck stock
- 4 tbsp Chinese rice wine, dry sherry or dry white wine
- 10-cm/4-inch piece fresh ginger, peeled and sliced
- 2 tbsp rice vinegar
- 2 tbsp soy sauce
- 2 tsp sesame oil
- 1 cinnamon stick
- 1 star anise pod
- 1 tsp white pepper
- 1 tsp salt
- 225 g/8 oz roast duck meat (preferably dark meat), shredded
- 175 g/6 oz fresh shiitake mushrooms, sliced
- 175 g/6 oz dried ramen noodles (flavouring sachet discarded, if included)
- 4 spring onions, sliced diagonally into 2.5-cm/1-inch pieces
- 4 eggs
- chilli oil, to garnish

Method

1. Soak the dried mushrooms in hot water for 30 minutes. Drain, reserving the liquid, and slice.

2. Combine the stock, wine, mushroom soaking liquid, ginger, vinegar, soy sauce, sesame oil, cinnamon stick, star anise and pepper and salt in a large saucepan. Bring to a simmer, then reduce the heat to low and simmer for 20 minutes. Strain the stock and discard the ginger slices. Return the stock, star anise and cinnamon stick to the pot. Bring back to a simmer and add the duck meat, the reserved soaked dried mushrooms and the fresh mushrooms. Simmer for a further 20 minutes, or until the mushrooms are tender. Remove the cinnamon stick and star anise, increase the heat and bring the soup back to the boil.

3. Add the noodles and cook, breaking them up with a spoon as needed, for about 3 minutes, or until tender. Stir in the spring onions.

4. Half-fill a medium-sized saucepan with water and bring the eggs to the boil over a high heat. Reduce the heat to low and carefully crack the eggs into the water. Cook for 4 minutes.

5. Ladle the soup into warmed bowls and top each with an egg. Garnish with a few drops of chilli oil and serve immediately.

POULTRY

ROAST CHICKEN WINGS WITH GARLIC

Serves: 4 **Prep: 25 mins** **Cook: 25 mins**

Ingredients

- 2 tbsp olive oil
- 1 tbsp runny honey
- 2 garlic cloves, crushed
- 3 tsp sumac
- 2 tsp sea salt flakes, crushed
- grated zest of 1 unwaxed lemon, plus 1 lemon, cut into wedges, to serve
- 500 g/1 lb 2 oz chicken wings, cut into drumettes and wingettes
- Greek-style natural yogurt, to serve

Method

1. Preheat the oven to 220°C/425°F/Gas Mark 7. Mix the oil, honey, garlic, sumac, salt and lemon zest together in a large roasting tin. Add the chicken and mix until well coated.

2. Roast the chicken at the top of the oven for 25 minutes, or until cooked through and slightly charred with a crispy skin, shaking the tin halfway through cooking to turn the pieces. Push a skewer into a chicken piece; the meat should no longer be pink and the juices should be clear and piping hot.

3. Leave the chicken to rest for 5 minutes. Serve with the Greek yogurt and lemon wedges for squeezing over.

POULTRY

CHICKEN NOODLE SOUP

Serves: 4 **Prep: 15 mins** **Cook: 25 mins**

Ingredients

1 tbsp groundnut oil

1 onion, finely chopped

2 celery sticks, finely chopped

1 large carrot, finely chopped

2 garlic cloves, crushed

400 g/14 oz skinless, boneless chicken breasts, cut into bite-sized pieces

150 g/5½ oz fine French beans, cut into 3-cm/1¼-inch pieces

1.2 litres/2 pints reduced-salt chicken stock

150 g/5½ oz dried wholemeal egg noodles

pepper (optional)

small bunch of fresh coriander leaves, to garnish

Method

1. Heat the oil in a saucepan over a medium heat. Add the onion, celery and carrot and cook, stirring occasionally, for 8 minutes, until soft but not brown.

2. Add the garlic and cook for 1 minute. Add the chicken to the pan with the beans, stock and pepper, if using. Bring to the boil, then reduce the heat and simmer for 5 minutes.

3. Add the noodles to the pan, bring back to a simmer and cook for 5 minutes, or until the noodles are just tender. Ladle the soup into warmed bowls and garnish with coriander leaves before serving.

POULTRY

TURKEY & LENTIL SOUP

Serves: 4 **Prep: 20 mins** **Cook: 55 mins**

Ingredients

- 1 tbsp olive oil
- 1 garlic clove, chopped
- 1 large onion, chopped
- 200 g/7 oz mushrooms, sliced
- 1 red pepper, deseeded and chopped
- 6 tomatoes, skinned, deseeded and chopped
- 1.2 litre/2 pints chicken stock
- 150 ml/5 fl oz red wine
- 85 g/3 oz cauliflower florets
- 1 carrot, peeled and chopped
- 200 g/7 oz red lentils
- 350 g/12 oz cooked turkey meat, chopped
- 1 courgette, trimmed and chopped
- 1 tbsp shredded fresh basil
- salt and pepper (optional)
- basil leaves, to garnish
- thick slices of fresh crusty bread, to serve

Method

1. Heat the oil in a large saucepan. Add the garlic and onion and cook over a medium heat, stirring, for 3 minutes, until slightly softened. Add the mushrooms, red pepper and tomatoes and cook for a further 5 minutes, stirring. Pour in the stock and red wine, then add the cauliflower, carrot and red lentils. Season with salt and pepper, if using. Bring to the boil, then lower the heat and simmer the soup gently for 25 minutes, until the vegetables are tender and cooked through.

2. Add the turkey and courgette to the pan and cook for 10 minutes. Stir in the shredded basil and cook for a further 5 minutes, then remove from the heat and ladle into warmed bowls. Garnish with basil leaves and serve with fresh crusty bread.

POULTRY

DUCK LEGS WITH OLIVES

Serves: 4 **Prep: 25 mins** **Cook: 1½–1¾ hours**

Ingredients

4 duck legs, all visible fat trimmed off

800 g/1 lb 12 oz canned chopped tomatoes

8 garlic cloves, peeled, but left whole

1 large onion, finely chopped

1 carrot, peeled and finely chopped

1 celery stick, peeled and finely chopped

3 fresh thyme sprigs

100 g/3½ oz Spanish green olives in brine, stuffed with pimientos, garlic or almonds, drained and rinsed

1 tsp finely grated orange rind

salt and pepper (optional)

Method

1. Put the duck legs in the base of a flameproof casserole or a large heavy-based frying pan with a tight-fitting lid. Add the tomatoes, garlic, onion, carrot, celery, thyme and olives and stir together. Season to taste with salt and pepper, if using.

2. Turn the heat to high and cook, uncovered, until the ingredients begin to bubble. Reduce the heat to low, cover tightly and simmer for 1¼–1½ hours, until the duck is very tender. Check occasionally and add a little water if the mixture appears to be drying out.

3. When the duck is tender, transfer it to a serving platter, cover and keep hot. Leave the casserole uncovered, increase the heat to medium and cook, stirring, for about 10 minutes, until the mixture forms a sauce. Stir in the orange rind, then taste and adjust the seasoning if necessary.

4. Mash the tender garlic cloves with a fork and spread over the duck legs. Spoon the sauce over the top. Serve at once.

POULTRY

CHICKEN SOUP WITH LEEKS & RICE

Serves: 6 **Prep: 15–20 mins, plus cooling** **Cook: 35–40 mins**

Ingredients

- 2 tbsp olive oil
- 3 leeks, chopped
- 6 skinless, boneless chicken thighs, diced
- 55 g/2 oz long-grain rice
- 1.3 litres/2¼ pints vegetable stock
- dash of Worcestershire sauce
- 6 fresh chives, snipped
- 6 thin bacon rashers
- 2 tbsp chopped fresh parsley
- salt and pepper (optional)

Method

1. Heat the oil in a saucepan. Add the leeks and cook over a low heat, stirring occasionally, for 5 minutes, until softened. Add the chicken, increase the heat to medium and cook, stirring frequently, for 2 minutes. Add the rice and cook, stirring constantly, for a further 2 minutes.

2. Pour in the stock, add the Worcestershire sauce and chives and bring to the boil. Reduce the heat, cover and simmer for 20–25 minutes. Check the chicken is tender and cooked through. Meanwhile, preheat the grill.

3. Grill the bacon for 2–4 minutes on each side, until crisp. Remove and leave to cool, then crumble.

4. Season the soup with salt and pepper to taste, if using, and stir in the parsley. Ladle into warmed bowls, sprinkle with the crumbled bacon and serve immediately.

POULTRY

CHICKEN & LENTIL SOUP

Serves: 6 **Prep: 15 mins** **Cook: 1½ hours–1 hour 35 mins**

Ingredients

3 tbsp olive oil
1 large onion, chopped
2 leeks, chopped
2 carrots, chopped
2 sticks celery, chopped
175 g/6 oz button mushrooms, chopped
4 tbsp dry white wine
1.2 litres/2 pints vegetable stock
1 bay leaf
2 tsp dried mixed herbs
175 g/6 oz Puy lentils
350 g/12 oz boneless cooked chicken, diced
salt and pepper (optional)

Method

1. Heat the oil in a large saucepan. Add the onion, leeks, carrots, celery and mushrooms and cook over a low heat, stirring occasionally, for 5–7 minutes, until softened but not coloured.

2. Increase the heat to medium, pour in the wine and cook for 2–3 minutes, until the alcohol has evaporated, then pour in the stock.

3. Bring to the boil, add the bay leaf and herbs, reduce the heat, cover and simmer for 30 minutes. Add the lentils, re-cover the pan and simmer, stirring occasionally, for a further 40 minutes, until they are tender.

4. Stir in the chicken, season to taste with salt and pepper, if using, and simmer for a further 5–10 minutes, until heated through. Ladle the soup into warmed bowls.

POULTRY

SAFFRON, CHICKEN & VEGETABLE STEW

Serves: 4 **Prep: 25 mins** **Cook: 45 mins**

Ingredients

- 1 tbsp olive oil
- 25 g/1 oz butter
- ½ onion, finely chopped
- 2 garlic cloves, finely chopped
- 1 leek, thinly sliced
- 300 g/10½ oz carrots, finely chopped
- pinch of saffron threads
- 100 ml/3½ fl oz boiling water
- 300 g/10½ oz skinless, boneless chicken thighs, halved
- 300 ml/10 fl oz hot chicken stock
- 175 g/6 oz baby leeks, halved lengthways
- 150 g/5½ oz baby carrots, halved lengthways
- juice of 1 lemon
- 2 tbsp finely chopped fresh flat-leaf parsley
- pinch of sea salt and a pinch of pepper (optional)

Method

1. Heat the oil and butter in a large saucepan over a medium heat until the butter stops foaming. Add the onion, garlic, thinly sliced leek and finely chopped carrots, reduce the heat to medium-low and cook for 10 minutes, covered, stirring occasionally.

2. Meanwhile, grind the saffron in a pestle and mortar, then add the boiling water, swirl and tip into a small bowl. Leave to steep.

3. Add the chicken, saffron water and stock to the vegetables and bring to the boil. Reduce the heat to low and simmer, covered, for 20 minutes. Add the baby leeks and baby carrots and cook for a further 10 minutes, or until the chicken is cooked through.

4. Stir in the lemon juice and parsley and season with the salt and pepper to taste, if using, and then serve.

POULTRY

CHICKEN WITH 40 GARLIC CLOVES

Serves: 4 **Prep: 18 mins** **Cook: 1 hour 20 mins**

Ingredients

1.5–2 kg/3 lb 5 oz–4 lb 8 oz whole chicken

½ lemon

40 whole garlic cloves, peeled

2 tbsp olive oil

4 fresh thyme sprigs

2 fresh rosemary sprigs

4 fresh parsley sprigs

1 large carrot, roughly chopped

2 celery sticks, roughly chopped

1 onion, roughly chopped

375 ml/13 fl oz white wine

salt and pepper (optional)

crusty French bread and a green salad, to serve

Method

1. Preheat the oven to 200°C/400°F/Gas Mark 6.
2. Stuff the chicken with the ½ lemon and four of the garlic cloves. Rub the chicken with a little of the oil and some salt and pepper, if using.
3. In a large flameproof casserole, spread out the remaining garlic cloves, the herbs, carrot, celery and onion, then place the chicken on top. Pour over the remaining oil and add the wine. Cover with a tight-fitting lid, place in the preheated oven and bake for 1¼ hours.
4. Remove the chicken from the casserole and check that it's cooked by inserting a skewer into the thickest part of the meat; the juices should run clear. Cover and keep warm. Remove the garlic cloves and reserve.
5. Place the casserole over a low heat and simmer the juices for 5 minutes to make a gravy. Strain, reserving the vegetables.
6. Carve the chicken and serve it with the vegetables from the casserole. Squeeze the flesh out of the garlic cloves and spread it on the bread. Serve immediately with the bread and a green salad.

POULTRY

BAKED CHICKEN & CHORIZO PAELLA

Serves: 4 **Prep: 20 mins** **Cook: 40 mins**

Ingredients

- 2 tbsp olive oil
- 100 g/3½ oz chorizo sausages, sliced
- 1 onion, finely chopped
- 1 red pepper, roughly chopped
- 400 g/14 oz boneless, skinless chicken thighs, cut into bite-sized pieces
- 4 large garlic cloves, finely chopped
- 350 g/12 oz paella rice
- 150 g/5½ oz frozen peas
- 1 tsp Spanish sweet paprika
- large pinch of saffron threads
- 125 ml/4 fl oz dry white wine
- 700 ml/1¼ pints chicken stock
- 200 g/7 oz large raw prawns, peeled
- salt and pepper (optional)
- chopped fresh parsley, to garnish
- lemon wedges, to serve

Method

1. Preheat the oven to 220°C/425°F/Gas Mark 7. Heat the oil in a flameproof casserole over a high heat. Reduce the heat to low–medium, add the chorizo and fry, stirring, for 3–4 minutes until it starts to brown and gives off its oil. Remove from the pan and pour off all but 2 tablespoons of the oil. Add the onion and red pepper and fry, stirring, for 3–5 minutes until soft. Add the chicken and garlic and stir until the chicken is coloured all over.

2. Add the rice and peas, stirring until the rice is coated in oil. Stir in the paprika and saffron threads, then add the wine and stock and season with salt and pepper, if using. Bring to the boil, stirring occasionally. Transfer to the preheated oven and bake, uncovered, for 15 minutes.

3. Remove from the oven and add the prawns and chorizo, pushing them down into the rice. Return to the oven and bake for a further 10 minutes, or until the rice is tender, the prawns are pink and cooked through and the chicken is cooked through. Cut into the middle of the chicken to check there are no remaining traces of pink. Garnish with parsley and serve with lemon wedges.

POULTRY

CREAM OF CHICKEN SOUP

Serves: 4 **Prep: 15 mins, plus cooling** **Cook: 40 mins**

Ingredients

3 tbsp butter

4 shallots, chopped

1 leek, sliced

450 g/1 lb skinless chicken breasts, chopped

600 ml/1 pint chicken stock

1 tbsp chopped fresh parsley

1 tbsp chopped fresh thyme, plus extra sprigs to garnish

175 ml/6 fl oz double cream

salt and pepper (optional)

Method

1. Melt the butter in a large saucepan over a medium heat. Add the shallots and cook, stirring, for 3 minutes, until slightly softened.

2. Add the leek and cook for a further 5 minutes, stirring.

3. Add the chicken, stock and herbs, and season to taste with salt and pepper, if using. Bring to the boil, then reduce the heat and simmer for 25 minutes, until the chicken is tender and cooked through. To check the chicken pieces are cooked through, cut into the middle to check that there are no remaining traces of pink or red.

4. Remove from the heat and leave to cool for 10 minutes. Transfer the soup to a food processor or blender and process until smooth (you may need to do this in batches).

5. Return the soup to the rinsed-out pan and warm over a low heat for 5 minutes.

6. Stir in the cream and cook for a further 2 minutes, then remove from the heat and ladle into warmed bowls. Garnish with thyme sprigs and serve immediately.

POULTRY

TURKEY & BARLEY STEW

Serves: 4   Prep: 20–25 mins   Cook: 35 mins

Ingredients

15 g/½ oz dried ceps

2 tbsp olive oil

1 onion, diced

450 g/1 lb button mushrooms, sliced

4 carrots, sliced

1 tsp salt

½ tsp pepper

200 g/7 oz barley

600 ml/1 pint vegetable stock

1 tbsp fresh thyme leaves

450 g/1 lb turkey breast meat

grated Parmesan cheese and chopped fresh parsley, to garnish

Method

1. Place the ceps in a small bowl and cover with hot water. Heat the oil in a large saucepan over a medium-high heat. Add the onion and cook, stirring frequently, for about 4 minutes until soft. Add the mushrooms and carrots to the pan with the salt and pepper. Cook, stirring occasionally, for 4 minutes until the vegetables are tender. Add the barley and stir to mix well. Add the stock.

2. Remove the ceps from the soaking water, reserving the soaking liquid, and chop. Add to the pan with the soaking liquid and bring to the boil. Meanwhile, finely chop the thyme and add to the pan. Reduce the heat to low and simmer, uncovered, for about 5 minutes.

3. Cut the turkey into 1-cm/½-inch cubes and add to the stew, stir to mix, then cover and simmer for 15 minutes, until the turkey is cooked through, the barley is tender, and most of the liquid has evaporated. Serve in bowls, garnished with the cheese and parsley.

POULTRY

CHICKEN CACCIATORE

Serves: 4 **Prep:** 30 mins **Cook:** 5 hours 30 mins

Ingredients

3 tbsp olive oil
4 skinless chicken portions
2 onions, sliced
2 garlic cloves, finely chopped
400 g/14 oz canned chopped tomatoes
1 tbsp tomato purée
2 tbsp chopped fresh parsley
2 tsp fresh thyme leaves
150 ml/5 fl oz red wine
salt and pepper (optional)
4 fresh thyme sprigs, to garnish

Method

1. This recipe requires a slow cooker. Heat the oil in a heavy-based frying pan. Add the chicken and cook over a medium heat, turning occasionally, for 10 minutes, until golden all over. Using a slotted spoon, transfer the chicken to the slow cooker.

2. Add the onions to the pan and cook, stirring occasionally, for 5 minutes, until soft and just turning golden. Add the garlic, tomatoes, tomato purée, parsley, thyme leaves and wine. Season with salt and pepper, if using, and bring to the boil.

3. Pour the tomato mixture over the chicken pieces. Cover and cook on low for 5 hours, until the chicken is tender and cooked through. Season with salt and pepper, if using. Transfer to warmed serving plates, garnish with the thyme sprigs and serve immediately.

POULTRY

STIR-FRIED TURKEY WITH CRANBERRY GLAZE

Serves: 4 **Prep: 15 mins** **Cook: 10 mins**

Ingredients

450 g/1 lb boneless turkey breast
2 tbsp sunflower oil
15 g/½ oz stem ginger
50 g/1¾ oz fresh or frozen cranberries
100 g/3½ oz canned chestnuts
4 tbsp cranberry sauce
3 tbsp light soy sauce
salt and pepper (optional)

Method

1. Remove any skin from the turkey breast. Using a sharp knife, thinly slice the turkey breast.

2. Heat the oil in a large preheated wok or frying pan. Add the turkey to the wok and stir-fry for 5 minutes, or until cooked through. Drain off the syrup from the stem ginger. Using a sharp knife, finely chop the ginger.

3. Add the ginger and the cranberries to the wok and stir-fry for 2–3 minutes, or until the cranberries have softened. Add the chestnuts, cranberry sauce and soy sauce, season with salt and pepper, if using, and bubble for 2–3 minutes.

4. Transfer to warmed serving dishes and serve immediately.

POULTRY

CHICKEN WITH GOAT'S CHEESE & MUSHROOM SAUCE

Serves: 4 **Prep: 15 mins** **Cook: 20 mins**

Ingredients

- 4 boneless, skinless chicken breasts, halved horizontally
- 2 tbsp olive oil
- 115 g/4 oz button mushrooms, sliced
- 1 tbsp unsalted butter
- 50 ml/2 fl oz chicken stock
- 125 ml/4 fl oz double cream
- 85 g/3 oz goat's cheese
- 15 g/½ oz fresh flat-leaf parsley, chopped
- salt and pepper (optional)

Method

1. Place the chicken between two pieces of clingfilm and pound with a meat mallet to a thickness of 5 mm/¼ inch. Season to taste with salt and pepper, if using.

2. Heat the oil in a large frying pan over a medium–high heat. Add the chicken and cook for about 3 minutes on each side, or until brown and cooked through. Transfer to a plate.

3. Add the mushrooms and butter to the pan and cook, stirring occasionally, until the liquid has evaporated, and the mushrooms are brown. Stir in the stock, cream, cheese and parsley. Bring to a simmer, add the chicken and cook until heated through. Season to taste with salt and pepper, if using, and serve immediately.

POULTRY

CHICKEN & SWEET POTATO BAKE

Serves: 4　　**Prep: 15 mins**　　**Cook: 35–40 mins**

Ingredients

- 2 sweet potatoes, peeled and cut into wedges
- 1 large courgette, sliced diagonally
- 1 red onion, cut into wedges
- 1 red pepper, deseeded and sliced
- 1 yellow pepper, deseeded and sliced
- 2 tbsp olive oil
- 1 tsp cumin seeds
- 4 chicken breasts, each weighing 150 g/5½ oz
- 2 tbsp pesto
- 12 cherry tomatoes
- 12 black olives
- 100 g/3½ oz kale, shredded
- 2 tbsp chopped fresh parsley, to garnish
- salt and pepper (optional)

Method

1. Preheat the oven to 200°C/400°F/Gas Mark 6.
2. Place the sweet potatoes, courgette, onion, red pepper and yellow pepper in a large roasting tin. Sprinkle over 1 tablespoon of the oil and the cumin seeds, season with salt and pepper, if using, and toss together until the vegetables are well coated with the oil. Roast in the preheated oven for 15 minutes.
3. Meanwhile, diagonally slash each chicken breast three times. Mix the remaining oil with the pesto and brush onto the chicken.
4. Remove the vegetables from the oven, add the tomatoes, olives and kale and toss, then place the chicken breasts on top.
5. Roast for a further 20–25 minutes, until the vegetables are slightly charred and the chicken is cooked through. Garnish with the chopped parsley before serving.

★ Variation

If you prefer fish, the chicken breast can be substituted with cod loins or salmon fillets – they will need less cooking time.

POULTRY

CHICKEN & APPLE POT

Serves: 4 **Prep: 30 mins** **Cook: 7 hours 55 mins**

Ingredients

1 tbsp olive oil

4 chicken portions, each weighing 175 g/6 oz

1 onion, chopped

2 celery sticks, roughly chopped

1½ tbsp plain flour

300 ml/10 fl oz clear apple juice

150 ml/5 fl oz chicken stock

1 cooking apple, cored and cut into quarters

2 bay leaves

1–2 tsp clear honey

1 yellow pepper, deseeded and cut into chunks

salt and pepper (optional)

To garnish

2 eating apples, cored and sliced

1 tbsp melted butter

2 tbsp demerara sugar

1 tbsp chopped fresh mint

Method

1. This recipe requires a slow cooker. Heat the oil in a heavy-based frying pan. Add the chicken and cook over a medium–high heat, turning frequently, for 10 minutes, until golden brown. Transfer to the slow cooker. Add the onion and celery to the pan and cook over a low heat for 5 minutes, until soft. Sprinkle in the flour and cook for 2 minutes, then remove from the heat.

2. Gradually stir in the apple juice and stock, then return to the heat and bring to the boil. Stir in the apple, bay leaves and honey and season with salt and pepper, if using. Pour the mixture over the chicken in the slow cooker, cover and cook on low for 6½ hours, until the chicken is tender and cooked through. Stir in the yellow pepper, re-cover and cook on high for 45 minutes.

3. Shortly before serving, preheat the grill. Brush one side of the eating apple slices with half the melted butter and sprinkle with half the sugar. Cook under the preheated grill for 2–3 minutes, until the sugar has caramelized. Turn the slices over with tongs, brush with the remaining butter and sprinkle with the remaining sugar. Grill for a further 2 minutes. Transfer the stew to warmed plates and garnish with the caramelized apple slices and the mint. Serve immediately.

POULTRY

CHICKEN & PUMPKIN CASSEROLE

Serves: 4 **Prep: 20 mins** **Cook: 1 hour 35 mins**

Ingredients

3 tbsp olive oil

2.25 kg/5 lb chicken, cut into 8 pieces and dusted in flour

200 g/7 oz fresh chorizo sausages, roughly sliced

small bunch of fresh sage leaves

1 onion, chopped

6 garlic cloves, sliced

2 celery sticks, sliced

1 small pumpkin or butternut squash, peeled, deseeded and roughly chopped

200 ml/7 fl oz dry sherry

600 ml/1 pint chicken stock

400 g/14 oz canned chopped tomatoes

2 bay leaves

salt and pepper (optional)

1 tbsp chopped fresh flat-leaf parsley, to garnish

Method

1. Preheat the oven to 180°C/350°F/Gas Mark 4.
2. Heat the oil in a flameproof casserole and cook the chicken, in batches, with the chorizo and sage leaves, until golden brown. Remove with a slotted spoon and reserve.
3. Add the onion, garlic, celery and pumpkin to the casserole and cook for 20 minutes, or until the mixture is golden brown.
4. Add the sherry, stock, tomatoes and bay leaves, and season to taste with salt and pepper, if using. Return the reserved chicken, chorizo and sage to the casserole. Cover and cook in the preheated oven for 1 hour.
5. Remove from the oven, stir in the parsley and serve immediately.

POULTRY

TURKEY STROGANOFF

Serves: 4 **Prep: 10 mins** **Cook: 25 mins**

Ingredients

- 3 tbsp sunflower oil
- 450 g/1 lb fresh turkey mince
- 30 g/1 oz butter
- 1 onion, very finely chopped
- 2 large garlic cloves, very finely chopped
- 250 g/9 oz chestnut mushrooms, trimmed and thinly chopped
- 4 tsp Dijon mustard
- pinch of freshly grated nutmeg
- 450 ml/16 fl oz soured cream
- 1 tsp freshly squeezed lemon juice, or to taste
- salt and pepper (optional)
- 4 tsp fresh flat-leaf parsley, coarsely chopped, to serve
- cooked tagliatelle, to serve

Method

1. Heat the oil in a large frying pan over a medium-high heat. Add the turkey and fry, stirring with a wooden spoon to break up the meat into large clumps, for 4–6 minutes until cooked through. Remove from the pan with a slotted spoon and set aside.

2. Pour off all but 1 tablespoon of the fat remaining in the pan. Add the butter and heat until melted. Add the onion and fry, stirring, for 3–5 minutes until soft. Stir in the garlic and mushrooms and season to taste with salt and pepper, if using. Fry, stirring, for about 5 minutes until the mushrooms re-absorb the liquid they give off.

3. Stir in the mustard and nutmeg, then return the turkey to the pan. Stir in the soured cream and bring to the boil, stirring. Reduce the heat and simmer for a few minutes until slightly reduced. Add lemon juice and adjust the seasoning, if using.

4. Divide the pasta between four plates and pour over the sauce. Sprinkle with parsley and serve immediately.

POULTRY

ITALIAN TURKEY STEW

Serves: 4 **Prep: 15 mins** **Cook: 50–60 mins**

Ingredients

- 1 tbsp olive oil
- 4 turkey escalopes or steaks
- 2 red peppers, deseeded and sliced
- 1 red onion, sliced
- 2 garlic cloves, finely chopped
- 300 ml/10 fl oz passata
- 150 ml/5 fl oz medium white wine
- 1 tbsp chopped fresh marjoram
- 400 g/14 oz canned cannellini beans, drained and rinsed
- 3 tbsp fresh white breadcrumbs
- salt and pepper (optional)
- fresh basil sprigs, to garnish

Method

1. Heat the oil in a flameproof casserole, add the turkey and cook over a medium heat for 5–10 minutes, turning occasionally, until browned all over. Transfer to a plate using a slotted spoon.

2. Add the red peppers and onion to the casserole and cook over a low heat, stirring occasionally, for 5 minutes, or until softened. Add the garlic and cook for a further 2 minutes.

3. Return the turkey to the casserole and add the passata, wine and marjoram. Season to taste with salt and pepper, if using. Bring to the boil, then reduce the heat, cover and simmer, stirring occasionally, for 25–30 minutes, or until the turkey is cooked through and tender. Meanwhile, preheat the grill to medium.

4. Stir the cannellini beans into the casserole and simmer for a further 5 minutes. Sprinkle the breadcrumbs over the top and place under the preheated grill for 2–3 minutes, or until golden. Serve immediately, garnished with basil sprigs.

POULTRY

DUCK JAMBALAYA STEW

Serves: 4 **Prep: 25 mins** **Cook: 35–40 mins**

Ingredients

- 4 duck breasts, about 150 g/5½ oz each
- 2 tbsp olive oil
- 225 g/8 oz gammon, cut into small chunks
- 225 g/8 oz chorizo, outer casing removed
- 1 onion, chopped
- 3 garlic cloves, chopped
- 3 celery sticks, chopped
- 1–2 fresh red chillies, deseeded and chopped
- 1 green pepper, deseeded and chopped
- 600 ml/1 pint chicken stock
- 1 tbsp chopped fresh oregano
- 400 g/14 oz canned chopped tomatoes
- 1–2 tsp hot pepper sauce, or to taste
- fresh flat-leaf parsley sprigs, to garnish
- green salad and cooked rice, to serve

Method

1. Remove and discard the skin and any fat from the duck breasts. Cut the flesh into bite-sized pieces.
2. Heat half the oil in a large deep frying pan and cook the duck, gammon and chorizo over a high heat, stirring frequently, for 5 minutes, or until browned all over. Using a slotted spoon, remove from the frying pan and set aside.
3. Heat the remaining oil in the frying pan then add the onion, garlic, celery and chilli and cook over a medium heat, stirring frequently, for 5 minutes, or until softened. Add the green pepper, then stir in the stock, oregano, tomatoes and hot pepper sauce.
4. Bring to the boil, then reduce the heat and return the duck, gammon and chorizo to the frying pan. Cover and simmer, stirring occasionally, for 20 minutes, or until the duck and gammon are tender.
5. Serve immediately, garnished with parsley sprigs and accompanied by a green salad and rice.

POULTRY

MEXICAN CHICKEN, CHILLI & POTATO POT

Serves: 4　　**Prep: 20 mins**　　**Cook: 35–40 mins**

Ingredients

2 tbsp vegetable oil

450 g/1 lb boneless, skinless chicken breasts, cubed

1 onion, finely chopped

1 green pepper, deseeded and finely chopped

1 potato, diced

1 sweet potato, diced

2 garlic cloves, very finely chopped

1–2 fresh green chillies, deseeded and finely chopped

200 g/7 oz canned chopped tomatoes

½ tsp dried oregano

½ tsp salt

4 tsp pepper

4 tbsp chopped fresh coriander

450 ml/16 fl oz chicken stock

Method

1. Heat the oil in a large heavy-based saucepan over a medium–high heat. Cook the chicken until lightly browned.

2. Reduce the heat to medium. Add the onion, green pepper, potato and sweet potato. Cover and cook for 5 minutes, stirring occasionally, until the vegetables begin to soften.

3. Add the garlic and chillies. Cook for 1 minute. Stir in the tomatoes, oregano, salt, pepper and half the coriander. Cook for 1 minute.

4. Pour in the stock. Bring to the boil, then cover and simmer over a low–medium heat for 15–20 minutes, or until the chicken is cooked through and the vegetables are tender.

5. Sprinkle with the remaining coriander just before serving.

POULTRY

HUNTER'S CHICKEN

Serves: 4 **Prep: 15–20 mins** **Cook: 1½ hours**

Ingredients

15 g/½ oz unsalted butter

2 tbsp olive oil

1.8 kg/4 lb skinned, unboned chicken portions

2 red onions, sliced

2 garlic cloves, finely chopped

400 g/14 oz canned chopped tomatoes

2 tbsp chopped fresh flat-leaf parsley

6 fresh basil leaves, torn

1 tbsp sun-dried tomato paste

150 ml/5 fl oz red wine

225 g/8 oz mushrooms, sliced

salt and pepper (optional)

Method

1. Preheat the oven to 160°C/325°F/Gas Mark 3. Heat the butter and oil in a flameproof casserole and cook the chicken over a medium-high heat, turning frequently, for 10 minutes, or until golden all over and sealed. Using a slotted spoon, transfer to a plate.

2. Add the onions and garlic to the casserole and cook over a low heat, stirring occasionally, for 10 minutes, or until softened and golden. Add the tomatoes with their juice, the herbs, sun-dried tomato paste and wine, and season to taste with salt and pepper, if using. Bring to the boil, then return the chicken portions to the casserole, pushing them down into the sauce.

3. Cover and cook in the preheated oven for 50 minutes. Add the mushrooms and cook for a further 10 minutes, or until the chicken is tender and the juices run clear when a skewer is inserted into the thickest part of the meat. Serve immediately.

POULTRY

COQ AU VIN

Serves: 4   **Prep: 20 mins**   **Cook: 1 hour 25 mins**

Ingredients

55 g/2 oz butter
2 tbsp olive oil
1.8 kg/4 lb chicken pieces
115 g/4 oz rindless smoked bacon, cut into strips
115 g/4 oz baby onions
115 g/4 oz chestnut mushrooms, halved
2 garlic cloves, finely chopped
2 tbsp brandy
225 ml/8 fl oz red wine
300 ml/10 fl oz chicken stock
1 bouquet garni
2 tbsp plain flour
salt and pepper (optional)
bay leaves, to garnish

Method

1. Melt half the butter with the oil in a large flameproof casserole. Add the chicken and cook over a medium heat, stirring, for 8–10 minutes, or until brown all over. Add the bacon, onions, mushrooms and garlic.

2. Pour in the brandy and set it alight with a match or taper. When the flames have died down, add the wine, stock and bouquet garni and season to taste with salt and pepper, if using. Bring to the boil, reduce the heat and simmer gently for 1 hour, or until the chicken is tender and the juices run clear when a skewer is inserted into the thickest part of the meat.

3. Remove and discard the bouquet garni. Transfer the chicken to a large plate and keep warm. Mix the flour with the remaining butter and whisk into the casserole, a little at a time. Bring to the boil, return the chicken to the casserole and heat through. Garnish with bay leaves and serve immediately (do not eat the bay leaves).

POULTRY

SPICED CHICKEN STEW

Serves: 6 **Prep: 10 mins** **Cook: 1½ hours**

Ingredients

- 1.8 kg/4 lb chicken pieces
- salt (optional)
- 2 tbsp paprika
- 2 tbsp olive oil
- 25 g/1 oz butter
- 450 g/1 lb onions, chopped
- 2 yellow peppers, deseeded and chopped
- 400 g/14 oz canned chopped tomatoes
- 225 ml/8 fl oz dry white wine
- 450 ml/16 fl oz chicken stock
- 1 tbsp Worcestershire sauce
- ½ tsp Tabasco sauce
- 1 tbsp finely chopped fresh flat-leaf parsley, plus extra to garnish
- 325 g/11½ oz canned sweetcorn kernels, drained
- 425 g/15 oz canned butter beans, drained and rinsed
- 2 tbsp plain flour
- 4 tbsp water

Method

1. Season the chicken pieces well with salt, if using, and dust with the paprika.

2. Heat the oil and butter in a flameproof casserole or large saucepan. Add the chicken pieces and cook over a medium heat, turning, for 10–15 minutes, or until browned all over. Transfer to a plate with a slotted spoon.

3. Add the onions and peppers to the casserole. Cook over a low heat, stirring occasionally, for 5 minutes, or until softened. Add the tomatoes, wine, stock, Worcestershire sauce, Tabasco sauce and parsley and bring to the boil, stirring. Return the chicken to the casserole, cover and simmer, stirring occasionally, for 30 minutes.

4. Add the sweetcorn and butter beans to the casserole, partially re-cover and simmer for a further 30 minutes, or until the chicken is tender and the juices run clear when a skewer is inserted into the thickest part of the meat. Place the flour and water in a small bowl and mix to make a paste. Stir a ladleful of the cooking liquid into the paste, then stir the paste into the stew. Cook, stirring frequently, for a further 5 minutes. Garnish with parsley and serve immediately.

CHICKEN & BARLEY STEW

Serves: 4 **Prep: 20–25 mins** **Cook: 1 hour 5 mins**

Ingredients

- 2 tbsp vegetable oil
- 8 small, skinless chicken thighs
- 500 ml/18 fl oz chicken stock
- 100 g/3½ oz pearl barley, rinsed and drained
- 200 g/7 oz small new potatoes, scrubbed and halved lengthways
- 2 large carrots, peeled and sliced
- 1 leek, trimmed and sliced
- 2 shallots, sliced
- 1 tbsp tomato purée
- 1 bay leaf
- 1 courgette, trimmed and sliced
- 2 tbsp chopped fresh flat-leaf parsley, plus extra sprigs to garnish
- 2 tbsp plain flour
- salt and pepper salt (optional)
- fresh crusty bread, to serve (optional)

Method

1. Heat the oil in a large pot over a medium heat. Add the chicken and cook for 3 minutes, then turn over and cook on the other side for a further 2 minutes. Add the stock, barley, potatoes, carrots, leek, shallots, tomato purée and bay leaf. Bring to the boil, lower the heat and simmer for 30 minutes.

2. Add the courgette and chopped parsley, cover the pan and cook for a further 20 minutes, or until the chicken is cooked through. Remove the bay leaf and discard.

3. Mix the flour with 4 tablespoons of water in a separate bowl, and stir into a smooth paste. Add it to the stew and cook, stirring, over a low heat for a further 5 minutes. Season to taste with salt and pepper, if using.

4. Remove from the heat, ladle into individual serving bowls and garnish with sprigs of fresh parsley. Serve with fresh crusty bread.

POULTRY

ROAST CHICKEN

Serves: 6 **Prep: 15 mins** **Cook: 2 hours 10 mins, plus resting**

Ingredients

1 chicken, weighing 2.25 kg/5 lb

55 g/2 oz butter, softened

2 tbsp chopped fresh lemon thyme, plus extra sprigs to garnish

1 lemon, cut into quarters

125 ml/4 fl oz white wine, plus extra if needed

salt and pepper (optional)

Method

1. Preheat the oven to 220°C/425°F/Gas Mark 7. Place the chicken in a roasting tin. Put the butter in a bowl, mix in the thyme, and salt and pepper to taste, if using, and use to butter the chicken.

2. Place the lemon inside the cavity. Pour the wine over and roast in the oven for 15 minutes.

3. Reduce the temperature to 190°C/375°F/Gas Mark 5 and roast, basting frequently, for a further 1¾ hours.

4. To check a whole bird is cooked through, pierce the thickest part of the leg between the drumstick and the thigh with a thin skewer. Any juices should be piping hot and clear. Transfer to a warmed platter, cover with foil and allow to rest for 10 minutes.

5. Simmer the pan juices in the roasting tin on the hob over a low heat until they have reduced and are thick and glossy. Season and reserve.

6. Place the chicken on a clean chopping board. Using a carving knife and fork, cut between the wings and the side of the breast. Remove the wings and cut slices off the breast.

7. Cut the legs from the body and cut through the joint to make drumsticks and thigh portions. Serve with the pan juices, garnished with thyme.

POULTRY

MOROCCAN-STYLE TURKEY

Serves: 4 **Prep: 20 mins** **Cook: 45–50 mins**

Ingredients

- 400 g/14 oz skinless, boneless turkey breasts, diced
- 1 onion, sliced
- 1 tsp ground cumin
- ½ tsp ground cinnamon
- 1 tsp hot chilli sauce
- 240 g/8½ oz canned chickpeas, drained and rinsed
- 600 ml/1 pint chicken stock
- 12 dried apricots
- 40 g/1½ oz cornflour
- 75 ml/2½ fl oz cold water
- 2 tbsp chopped fresh coriander
- cooked couscous or rice, to serve

Method

1. Put the turkey, onion, cumin, cinnamon, chilli sauce, chickpeas and stock into a large saucepan or frying pan and bring to the boil. Reduce the heat, cover and simmer for 15 minutes.

2. Stir in the apricots and return to the boil. Reduce the heat, cover and simmer for a further 15 minutes, or until the turkey is thoroughly cooked and tender.

3. Blend the cornflour with the water in a small bowl and stir into the casserole. Return to the boil, stirring constantly, and cook until the casserole thickens. Reduce the heat, cover and simmer for a further 5 minutes..

4. Stir half of the coriander into the casserole. Transfer to a warmed serving dish and sprinkle over the remaining coriander. Serve immediately, with cooked couscous.

★ Variation

Try serving baked sweet jacket potatoes with this casserole instead of the couscous. Their flavour will complement the spicy sweetness of the dish.

POULTRY

MEAT

GINGER PORK WITH SHIITAKE MUSHROOMS	58
SPRING LAMB STEW	60
BEER-BRAISED BEEF SHORT RIBS	62
LARGE MIXED GRILL	64
PORK MEDALLIONS IN A CREAMY SAUCE	66
CHORIZO & BLUE CHEESE OMELETTE	68
CHESTNUT & PANCETTA SOUP	69
HEARTY BEEF STEW	70
PORK STIR-FRY WITH CASHEWS, LIME & MINT	72
PORK HOT POT	74
ONE-POT LASAGNE	76
CHUNKY POTATO & BEEF SOUP	78
HAM & LENTIL SOUP	79
TAGINE OF LAMB	80
BEEF IN BLACK BEAN SAUCE	81
MEDITERRANEAN LAMB WITH APRICOTS & PISTACHIOS	82
KASHMIRI LAMB & FENNEL STEW	84
CHILLI CON CARNE	86
RATATOUILLE SAUSAGE BAKE	88
COUNTRY-STYLE HAM WITH PINTO BEANS	90
BEEF IN BEER WITH HERB DUMPLINGS	92
LAMB PILAF	94
CHORIZO WITH BARLEY & BUTTER BEANS	96
PORK WITH MIXED GREEN BEANS	97
SAUSAGE & BEAN CASSEROLE	98
BEEF & VEGETABLE STEW WITH CORN	100
TEXAS LONE-STAR CHILLI	102
CINNAMON LAMB CASSEROLE	104

GINGER PORK WITH SHIITAKE MUSHROOMS

Serves: 4 **Prep: 15 mins** **Cook: 8–10 mins**

Ingredients

2 tbsp vegetable oil

3 shallots, finely chopped

2 garlic cloves, crushed

5-cm/2-inch piece fresh ginger, thinly sliced

500 g/1 lb 2 oz pork stir-fry strips

250 g/9 oz shiitake mushrooms, sliced

4 tbsp soy sauce

4 tbsp rice wine

1 tsp light muscovado sugar

1 tsp cornflour

2 tbsp cold water

chopped fresh coriander, to garnish

Method

1. Heat a wok over a high heat, then add the oil. Add the shallots and stir-fry for 2–3 minutes, then add the garlic and ginger and stir-fry for 1 minute.

2. Add the pork strips and stir-fry for a further minute, then add the mushrooms and stir-fry for 2–3 minutes until the pork is cooked through.

3. Stir in the soy sauce, rice wine and sugar. Blend the cornflour and water until smooth, add to the pan, stirring, and cook until the juices are thickened and clear. Transfer to warmed serving dishes, garnish with coriander and serve immediately.

MEAT

SPRING LAMB STEW

Serves: 4 **Prep: 20 mins** **Cook: 1½ hours –1 hour 40 mins**

Ingredients

40 g/1½ oz butter

2 tbsp sunflower oil, plus extra as needed

900 g/2 lb boned shoulder of lamb, trimmed and cut into large chunks, any bones reserved

2 shallots, finely chopped

1 tbsp sugar

1 litre/1¾ pints lamb stock

2 tbsp tomato purée

1 bouquet garni, with several parsley and thyme sprigs, 1 bay leaf and 1 small rosemary sprig

8 new potatoes, such as Charlotte, scrubbed and halved, if large

4 young turnips, quartered

12 baby carrots, scrubbed

140 g/5 oz frozen peas

salt and pepper (optional)

chopped fresh flat-leaf parsley, to garnish

baguette, to serve (optional)

Method

1. Melt 30 g/1 oz of the butter with the oil in a large frying pan over a medium heat. Add the lamb, in batches, and fry, stirring, until coloured on all sides, adding extra oil, if necessary. Transfer the meat to a large casserole as it colours.

2. Melt the remaining butter with the fat left in the pan. Add the shallots and stir for 3 minutes, or until beginning to soften. Sprinkle with the sugar, increase the heat and continue stirring until the shallots caramelize, ensuring that they do not burn. Transfer to the casserole and remove any charred bits from the frying pan base. Add half of the stock and bring to the boil, scraping the pan base, then tip this mixture into the casserole.

3. Add the remaining stock, tomato purée, bouquet garni and bones, if any, to the casserole. Season with salt and pepper, if using. Cover and bring to the boil. Reduce the heat and simmer for 45 minutes.

4. Add the potatoes, turnips and carrots and simmer for 15 minutes. Add the peas, uncover and simmer for a further 5–10 minutes, or until the meat and all the vegetables are tender. Remove and discard the bones, if used, and the bouquet garni. Taste and adjust the seasoning, if necessary. Garnish with parsley and serve with a baguette for soaking up the juices, if liked.

MEAT

BEER-BRAISED BEEF SHORT RIBS

Serves: 4 **Prep: 20–25 mins** **Cook: 2 hours 35 mins–3 hours 5 mins**

Ingredients

- 6 fresh thyme sprigs
- 6 fresh oregano sprigs
- 3 fresh rosemary sprigs
- 3 tbsp olive oil
- 900 g/2 lb thin ribs of beef (bone in), cut into 8 pieces
- 2 carrots, roughly chopped
- 1 onion, roughly chopped
- 2 celery sticks, roughly chopped
- 2 garlic cloves, crushed
- 350 ml/12 fl oz beer, at room temperature
- 425 g/15 oz canned tomato purée
- 225 ml/8 fl oz beef stock
- rock salt and pepper (optional)
- fresh flat-leaf parsley, finely chopped, to garnish

Method

1. Preheat the oven to 140°/275°F/Gas Mark 1 and make a bouquet garni by tying the herb sprigs together with string.

2. Heat 2 tablespoons of the oil in a casserole over a medium-high heat. Generously season the meat all over with salt and pepper, if using.

3. When the oil is very hot, add the ribs to the casserole in batches. Cook, turning occasionally, for about 8 minutes, until brown all over. Remove the ribs and pour the fat out of the casserole.

4. Add the remaining oil to the casserole and heat over a medium-high heat. Add the carrots, onion and celery and cook for about 3 minutes, until they are beginning to brown. Stir in the garlic and cook for a further minute.

5. Add the beer and bring to the boil, stirring and scraping up the sediment from the casserole base. Boil for 3–5 minutes, until the beer is reduced by half. Stir in the tomato purée and stock. Return the ribs to the casserole and add the bouquet garni.

6. Bring to the boil, cover and transfer to the oven. Cook for 2–2½ hours until the meat is very tender.

7. Before serving, remove and discard the bouquet garni. Serve garnished with chopped parsley.

MEAT

LARGE MIXED GRILL

Serves: 2 **Prep: 15 mins** **Cook: 27–31 mins**

Ingredients

1 fillet steak, about 225 g/8 oz

2 small lamb chops

2 large field mushrooms

1 large beef tomato, cut in half

6 tbsp vegetable oil

2 pork sausages

1 gammon steak, about 225 g/8 oz

55 g/2 oz chorizo, sliced

2 eggs

salt and pepper (optional)

cooked chips, to serve

Method

1. Season the fillet steak, lamb chops, mushrooms and tomato with salt and pepper, if using.

2. Heat 4 tablespoons of the oil over a high heat in a large frying pan. When the oil starts to smoke, add the lamb chops and sausages and cook the chops for 2 minutes on each side until brown. Reduce the heat and cook the chops to your liking. Then remove the chops from the pan and keep warm on a large serving platter.

3. Return the heat to high and add the steaks. Cook the gammon for 3–4 minutes on each side and the fillet steak for 2 minutes on each side. Turn the sausages every now and then.

4. Remove the gammon and fillet steaks from the pan and add to the platter. Add the chorizo, mushrooms and tomato and cook on each side for 4 minutes, then add to the platter, leaving the sausages in the pan.

5. Reduce the heat to medium and heat the remaining 2 tablespoons of oil. Fry the eggs and add to the platter. Remove the sausages from the frying pan, slicing one open to ensure that no traces of pink remain.

6. Cut the gammon and fillet steaks in half and serve the platter immediately, with freshly cooked chips, if liked.

MEAT

PORK MEDALLIONS IN A CREAMY SAUCE

Serves: 4 **Prep: 20 mins** **Cook: 15–20 mins**

Ingredients

500 g/1 lb 2 oz pork fillet
1 tbsp olive oil
15 g/½ oz butter
1 onion, finely chopped
200 ml/7 fl oz dry cider
1 tbsp Dijon mustard
150 ml/5 fl oz crème fraîche
salt and pepper (optional)
1 tbsp chopped fresh flat-leaf parsley, to garnish

Method

1. Trim the pork fillet of any fat, then cut into 2.5-cm/1-inch thick slices. Place between two sheets of clingfilm and beat with a meat mallet until the meat is about half its original thickness. Lightly season on both sides with salt and pepper, if using.

2. Heat the oil and butter in a wide frying pan, add the pork slices and fry over a medium-high heat for 3–4 minutes, turning once, until golden brown. Remove from the pan, set aside and keep warm.

3. Add the onion to the pan and fry gently, stirring, for 3–4 minutes, until soft. Add the cider, stirring with a wooden spoon to scrape up any sediment from the base of the pan, then boil rapidly for about 1 minute until slightly reduced. Stir in the mustard and crème fraîche, and gently simmer, stirring, until the sauce is smooth and has thickened a little.

4. Return the pork medallions to the pan and bring the sauce back to the boil. Season to taste with salt and pepper, if using, sprinkle with chopped parsley and serve immediately.

MEAT

CHORIZO & BLUE CHEESE OMELETTE

Serves: 2 **Prep:** 15 mins plus cooling **Cook:** 20 mins

Ingredients

- 1 tbsp olive oil
- 1 tbsp butter
- 200 g/7 oz chorizo, diced
- 1 large red onion, chopped
- 5 large eggs, beaten
- 150 g/5½ oz blue cheese, crumbled
- pepper (optional)

Method

1. Preheat the grill to high.
2. Heat the oil and butter in a large frying pan over a medium heat. Add the chorizo and red onion and fry, stirring, for 8–10 minutes, or until golden.
3. Pour in the eggs and season to taste with pepper, if using. Using a spatula, scrape the eggs away from the edges of the pan in a circular motion until the omelette starts to set.
4. Scatter over the cheese and place under the preheated grill for 5 minutes, or until golden and bubbling.
5. Remove from the grill and leave to cool for 5 minutes before serving.

MEAT

CHESTNUT & PANCETTA SOUP

Serves: 6 **Prep: 15 mins** **Cook: 45–50 mins**

Ingredients

3 tbsp olive oil

175 g/6 oz pancetta, cut into strips

2 onions, finely chopped

2 carrots, finely chopped

2 sticks celery, finely chopped

350 g/12 oz dried chestnuts, soaked overnight

2 cloves of garlic, finely chopped

1 tbsp finely chopped fresh rosemary

1 litre/1¾ pints chicken stock

salt and pepper (optional)

2 tbsp extra virgin olive oil, for drizzling

toasted bread to serve (optional)

Method

1. Heat the olive oil in a large saucepan, add the pancetta and cook over a medium heat, stirring frequently, for 2–3 minutes, until starting to brown.
2. Add the onions, carrots and celery and cook, stirring frequently, for 10 minutes, or until slightly golden and softened.
3. Drain the chestnuts, add to the saucepan with the garlic and rosemary, and stir well. Pour in the stock, bring to a simmer and cook, uncovered, for 30–35 minutes, until the chestnuts are beginning to soften and break down.
4. Season to taste with salt and pepper, if using. Ladle the soup into warmed bowls, drizzle with extra virgin olive oil and serve immediately, with toasted bread, if using.

MEAT

HEARTY BEEF STEW

Serves: 4 **Prep: 20–25 mins** **Cook: 2½ hours– 2 hours 40 mins,** plus standing

Ingredients

- 1.3 kg/3 lb boneless braising steak, cut into 5-cm/2-inch pieces
- 2 tbsp vegetable oil
- 2 onions, cut into 2.5 cm/1-inch pieces
- 3 tbsp plain flour
- 3 garlic cloves, finely chopped
- 1 litre/1¾ pints beef stock
- 3 carrots, cut into 2.5 cm/1-inch lengths
- 2 celery sticks, cut into 2.5 cm/1-inch lengths
- 1 tbsp tomato ketchup
- 1 bay leaf
- ¼ tsp dried thyme
- ¼ tsp dried rosemary
- 1 tsp salt
- 900 g/2 lb Maris Piper potatoes, cut into large chunks
- additional salt and pepper (optional)

Method

1. Season the steak generously with salt and pepper, if using. Heat the oil in a large flameproof casserole over a high heat. When the oil begins to smoke slightly, add the steak, in batches, and cook, stirring, for 5–8 minutes, until well browned. Using a slotted spoon, transfer to a bowl.

2. Reduce the heat to medium, add the onions and cook, stirring occasionally, for 5 minutes, until translucent. Stir in the flour and cook, stirring constantly, for 2 minutes. Add the garlic and cook for 1 minute. Whisk in 225 ml/8 fl oz of the stock and cook, scraping up the sediment from the casserole base, then stir in the remaining stock and add the carrots, celery, ketchup, bay leaf, thyme, rosemary and 1 teaspoon of salt. Return the steak to the casserole.

3. Bring back to a simmer, cover and cook over a low heat for 1 hour. Add the potatoes, re-cover the casserole and simmer for 30 minutes. Remove the lid, increase the heat to medium and cook, stirring occasionally, for 30 minutes, or until the contents are tender.

4. If the stew becomes too thick, add a little more stock or water and adjust the seasoning. Leave to stand for 15 minutes before serving.

MEAT

PORK STIR-FRY WITH CASHEWS, LIME & MINT

Serves: 2 **Prep: 20–25 mins** **Cook: 10 mins**

Ingredients

- 280 g/10 oz pork fillet
- 1 tsp coriander seeds
- ½ tsp white peppercorns
- ¼ tsp salt
- ¼ tsp sugar
- juice and finely grated rind of 1 lime
- 2 tbsp groundnut oil
- 1 tsp finely chopped fresh ginger
- 1 garlic clove, thinly sliced
- 3 spring onions, white and green parts separated, then halved lengthways and sliced into 2-cm/¾-inch pieces
- 1 small green pepper, deseeded and thinly sliced
- 2 tbsp cashew nuts, roughly chopped
- 1 tbsp chicken stock
- 1 tsp Thai fish sauce
- 2 tbsp fresh mint, to garnish

Method

1. Diagonally slice the pork across the grain into thin bite-sized pieces. Flatten with the back of a knife or with a meat mallet. Using a mortar and pestle, crush together the coriander seeds, peppercorns, salt, sugar and lime rind. Spread the mixture over both sides of the pork, pressing it in well. Leave to stand for 15 minutes.

2. Heat a wok over a high heat, then add 1 tablespoon of the oil. Add the pork and stir-fry for 2–3 minutes, until cooked through. Transfer to a plate with the juices. Wipe out the wok with kitchen paper.

3. Heat the wok over a medium–high heat, then add the remaining oil. Add the ginger and garlic and stir-fry for a few seconds. Add the white spring onion and green pepper and stir-fry for 2 minutes. Add the cashew nuts and stir-fry for a further minute.

4. Increase the heat to high, then return the pork and juices to the wok. Add the stock, lime juice, Thai fish sauce and green spring onion. Stir-fry for 30 seconds to heat through, then sprinkle with the mint and serve.

MEAT

PORK HOT POT

Serves: 4   **Prep: 20 mins**   **Cook: 1 hour 20 mins**

Ingredients

85 g/3 oz plain flour

1.3 kg/3 lb pork fillet, cut into 5-mm/¼-inch slices

4 tbsp sunflower oil

2 onions, thinly sliced

2 garlic cloves, finely chopped

400 g/14 oz canned chopped tomatoes

350 ml/12 fl oz dry white wine

1 tbsp torn fresh basil leaves

2 tbsp chopped fresh parsley

salt and pepper (optional)

fresh oregano, to garnish

fresh crusty bread, to serve

Method

1. Spread the flour on a plate and season with salt and pepper. Coat the pork slices in the flour, shaking off any excess. Heat the oil in a casserole. Add the pork slices and cook over a medium heat, turning occasionally, for 4–5 minutes, or until brown. Transfer to a plate with a slotted spoon.

2. Add the onion slices to the casserole and cook over a low heat, stirring occasionally, for 10 minutes, or until golden brown. Add the garlic and cook for a further 2 minutes, then add the tomatoes, wine and basil and season to taste with salt and pepper, if using. Cook, stirring frequently, for 3 minutes.

3. Return the pork to the casserole, cover and simmer gently for 1 hour, or until the meat is tender. Stir in the parsley, garnish with oregano and serve with fresh crusty bread.

★ Variation

Preheat the oven to 160°C/325°F/Gas Mark 3. Layer slices of apple over the casserole after returning the pork in step 3. Add knobs of butter over the top. Place the lid over the casserole and bake for 1½ hours, instead of simmering. Remove the lid for the last 30 minutes.

MEAT

ONE-POT LASAGNE

Serves: 4 **Prep: 8 mins** **Cook: 35–40 mins**

Ingredients

1 tbsp olive oil

1 onion, diced

600 g/1 lb 5 oz fresh beef mince

400 g/14 oz canned chopped tomatoes

100 ml/3½ fl oz beef stock

1 tbsp tomato purée

1 tsp dried oregano

2 courgettes

175 g/6 oz cream cheese

175 g/6 oz natural yogurt

400 g/14 oz mozzarella cheese, sliced or grated

Method

1. Heat the oil in a deep frying pan, add the onion and sauté for 4–5 minutes.

2. Add the mince and cook, breaking it up with a wooden spoon, for 3–4 minutes, until brown all over.

3. Add the chopped tomatoes and stock, then stir in the tomato purée and oregano. Bring to a simmer and cook for 15–20 minutes, until most of the moisture has been absorbed.

4. Meanwhile, using a vegetable peeler, slice the courgettes into thin strips and place them in a colander. Pour over boiling water, then leave to drain.

5. Remove half the mince from the pan and set aside. Layer half the courgette slices over the mince remaining in the pan. Spoon over the reserved mince and cover with the remaining courgette slices.

6. Preheat the grill to hot. Whisk together the cream cheese and yogurt and spread the mixture over the courgette slices. Top with the cheese, then cook under the grill for 10–12 minutes, until golden and bubbling. Serve immediately.

MEAT

CHUNKY POTATO & BEEF SOUP

Serves: 4 **Prep: 20 mins** **Cook: 35 mins**

Ingredients

2 tbsp vegetable oil

225 g/8 oz lean braising steak, cut into strips

225 g/8 oz new potatoes, halved

1 carrot, diced

2 celery sticks, sliced

2 leeks, sliced

850 ml/1½ pints beef stock

8 baby sweetcorn cobs, sliced

1 bouquet garni

2 tbsp dry sherry

salt and pepper (optional)

chopped fresh flat-leaf parsley, to garnish

Method

1. Heat the oil in a large saucepan. Add the strips of meat to the pan and cook for 3 minutes, turning constantly. Add the potatoes, carrot, celery and leeks, and cook for a further 5 minutes, stirring.

2. Pour the stock into the pan and bring to the boil. Reduce the heat until the liquid is simmering, then add the sweetcorn and the bouquet garni. Cook for a further 20 minutes, or until cooked through.

3. Remove and discard the bouquet garni. Stir the sherry into the soup and season to taste with salt and pepper, if using.

4. Ladle the soup into warmed bowls, garnish with chopped parsley and serve immediately.

MEAT

HAM & LENTIL SOUP

79

Serves: 2 **Prep: 10 mins** **Cook: 25–30 mins**

Ingredients

200 g/7 oz cooked ham

1 tbsp vegetable oil

1 onion, finely chopped

1 clove of garlic, finely chopped

1 carrot, finely diced

1 stick celery, thinly sliced

400 g/14 oz canned cooked green lentils, drained

1 tsp finely chopped fresh rosemary leaves

600 ml/1 pint vegetable or ham stock

pepper (optional)

Method

1. Using two forks, finely shred the cooked ham and set aside.
2. Heat the oil in a saucepan over a medium-high heat. Add the onion, garlic, carrot and celery and sauté for 4–5 minutes, or until starting to soften.
3. Add the cooked lentils, rosemary, shredded ham and stock, and season to taste with pepper, if using. Cover and simmer for 20 minutes, or until the vegetables are just tender. Ladle the soup into warm bowls and serve.

MEAT

TAGINE OF LAMB

Serves: 4 **Prep: 25 mins** **Cook: 1 hour 40 mins**

Ingredients

350 g/12 oz boneless lamb, trimmed of fat
1 tbsp sunflower or corn oil
1 onion, chopped
1 garlic clove, chopped
600 ml/1 pint vegetable stock
grated rind and juice of 1 orange
1 tsp honey and 1 cinnamon stick
1-cm/½-inch piece fresh ginger, finely chopped
2 tbsp fresh coriander
1 aubergine
4 tomatoes
115 g/4 oz dried apricots
salt and pepper (optional)
cooked couscous, to serve

Method

1. Cut the lamb into 2.5-cm/1-inch cubes. Heat the oil in a large heavy-based frying pan or flameproof casserole over a medium heat. Add the onion and lamb and cook, stirring frequently, for 5 minutes, or until the meat is lightly browned all over.

2. Add the garlic, stock, orange rind and juice, honey, cinnamon stick and ginger. Bring to the boil, then reduce the heat, cover and leave to simmer for 45 minutes. Meanwhile, chop the coriander.

3. Using a sharp knife, halve the aubergine lengthways and slice thinly. Peel and chop the tomatoes. Add the aubergine to the frying pan with the tomatoes and apricots. Cover and cook for a further 45 minutes, or until the lamb is tender.

4. Stir in the coriander and season to taste with salt and pepper, if using. Serve immediately with couscous.

MEAT

BEEF IN BLACK BEAN SAUCE

Serves: 4 **Prep: 15 mins** **Cook: 8–10 mins**

Ingredients

3 tbsp groundnut oil

450 g/1 lb beef sirloin, thinly sliced

1 red pepper, deseeded and thinly sliced

1 green pepper, deseeded and thinly sliced

6 spring onions, sliced

2 garlic cloves, crushed

1 tbsp grated fresh ginger

2 tbsp black bean sauce

1 tbsp sherry

1 tbsp soy sauce

Method

1. Heat 2 tablespoons of the oil in a wok and add the beef. Stir-fry over a high heat for 1–2 minutes. Remove from the wok and set aside.
2. Add the remaining oil, then add the red and green peppers and stir-fry for 2 minutes. Add the spring onions, garlic and ginger and stir-fry for 30 seconds.
3. Add the black bean sauce, sherry and soy sauce, then stir in the beef and heat until bubbling.
4. Transfer to warmed bowls and serve immediately.

MEAT

MEDITERRANEAN LAMB WITH APRICOTS & PISTACHIOS

Serves: 4　　**Prep: 25 mins, plus standing**　　**Cook: 1½ hours**

Ingredients

- pinch of saffron threads
- 2 tbsp almost-boiling water
- 450 g/1 lb lean, boneless lamb, such as leg steaks
- 1½ tbsp plain flour
- 1 tsp ground coriander
- ½ tsp ground cumin
- ½ tsp ground allspice
- 1 tbsp olive oil
- 1 onion, chopped
- 2–3 garlic cloves, chopped
- 450 ml/16 fl oz lamb or chicken stock
- 1 cinnamon stick, bruised
- 85 g/3 oz dried apricots, roughly chopped
- 175 g/6 oz courgettes, sliced
- 115 g/4 oz cherry tomatoes
- 1 tbsp chopped fresh coriander
- salt and pepper (optional)
- 2 tbsp roughly chopped pistachio nuts, to garnish
- couscous, to serve

Method

1. Put the saffron threads in a heatproof jug with the water and leave for at least 10 minutes to infuse. Trim off any fat or gristle from the lamb and cut into 2.5-cm/1-inch chunks. Mix the flour and spices together, then toss the lamb in the spiced flour until well coated and reserve any remaining spiced flour.

2. Heat the oil in a large, heavy-based saucepan and cook the onion and garlic, stirring frequently, for 5 minutes, or until softened. Add the lamb and cook over a high heat, stirring frequently, for 3 minutes, or until browned on all sides and sealed. Sprinkle in the reserved spiced flour and cook, stirring constantly, for 2 minutes, then remove from the heat.

3. Gradually stir in the stock and the saffron and its soaking liquid, then return to the heat and bring to the boil, stirring. Add the cinnamon stick and apricots. Reduce the heat, cover and simmer, stirring occasionally, for 1 hour.

4. Add the courgettes and tomatoes and cook for a further 15 minutes. Discard the cinnamon stick. Stir in the coriander and season to taste with salt and pepper, if using. Serve sprinkled with the pistachio nuts, accompanied by couscous.

MEAT

KASHMIRI LAMB & FENNEL STEW

Serves: 4 **Prep: 20 mins** **Cook: 2 hours -2 hours 15 mins**

Ingredients

- 4 tbsp vegetable or groundnut oil
- 2 onions, halved and thinly sliced
- 600 g/1 lb 5 oz lamb shoulder, trimmed and cut into bite-sized pieces
- 4 garlic cloves, crushed
- 2 tsp finely grated fresh ginger
- 1 tbsp ground coriander
- 1 tsp Kashmiri chilli powder
- 1 tsp salt
- 300 g/10½ oz potatoes, halved
- 500 ml/18 fl oz lamb or chicken stock
- 200 ml/7 fl oz single cream
- 4 tbsp ground almonds
- 2 tbsp crushed fennel seeds
- 6 tbsp finely chopped fresh coriander
- 2 tbsp finely chopped fresh mint

Method

1. Heat the oil in a non-stick saucepan, add the onions and cook over a low heat, stirring frequently, for about 15–20 minutes, until lightly browned.

2. Increase the heat to high, add the lamb and stir-fry for 4–5 minutes, until sealed. Reduce the heat to medium and add the garlic, ginger, ground coriander, chilli powder and salt. Stir and cook for a further 1–2 minutes.

3. Add the potatoes and stock, then cover and simmer over a low heat for about 1½ hours, or until the lamb is tender.

4. Uncover the pan, increase the heat slightly and stir in the cream and ground almonds. Cook for a further 8–10 minutes, until thickened and reduced. Take care not to boil or the cream will split.

5. Add the crushed fennel seeds to the pan and cook for a further 3–4 minutes. Remove from the heat and stir in the fresh coriander and mint. Serve immediately.

MEAT

CHILLI CON CARNE

Serves: 4 **Prep: 15–20 mins** **Cook: 45 mins**

Ingredients

1 tbsp rapeseed oil

400 g/14 oz fresh lean beef mince (10 per cent fat)

1 large onion, finely chopped

2 celery sticks, chopped

3 garlic cloves, finely chopped

1 large green pepper, deseeded and roughly chopped

400 g/14 oz canned chopped tomatoes

1 tbsp tomato purée

30 g/1 oz chilli pesto

1–2 tsp crushed dried chillies

½ tsp ground coriander

½ tsp ground cumin

1 tsp salt

pepper (optional)

300 g/10½ oz brown basmati rice

200 g/7 oz mushrooms, sliced

400 g/14 oz canned red kidney beans, drained and rinsed

chopped fresh flat-leaf parsley, to garnish

Method

1. Heat the oil in a large non-stick frying pan over a medium–high heat. Add the beef and cook, stirring occasionally, for a few minutes, until brown all over.

2. Push the beef to the side of the pan, then add the onion, celery and garlic. Reduce the heat to medium–low, cover and cook for 5 minutes, until the vegetables are soft but not brown.

3. Stir in the green pepper, tomatoes, tomato purée, pesto, chillies, coriander, cumin, ½ teaspoon of the salt, and pepper, if using. Bring to a simmer, reduce the heat to very low, then re-cover and cook for 25 minutes.

4. Meanwhile, cook the rice with the remaining salt according to the packet instructions until tender, then drain.

5. Add the mushrooms and kidney beans to the beef mixture and stir. Bring back to a simmer and cook for a further 5 minutes. Garnish the chilli with the parsley and serve immediately with the rice.

MEAT

RATATOUILLE SAUSAGE BAKE

Serves: 4 **Prep: 12 mins** **Cook: 55 mins–1 hour 10 mins**

Ingredients

½ tbsp olive oil
450 g/1 lb sausages
1 red pepper, deseeded and chopped
1 yellow pepper, deseeded and chopped
1 red onion, cut into wedges
1 small aubergine, cubed
2 courgettes, thickly sliced
400 ml/14 fl oz cider
salt and pepper (optional)

Method

1. Preheat the oven to 180°C/350°F/Gas Mark 4.
2. Heat the oil in a large casserole, add the sausages and cook until brown all over. Remove from the casserole with a slotted spoon and set aside.
3. Add the red pepper, yellow pepper, onion, aubergine and courgettes to the casserole and stir-fry for 5–6 minutes.
4. Return the sausages to the casserole, add the cider, season to taste with salt and pepper, if using, and bring to a simmer.
5. Cover and cook in the preheated oven for 30 minutes.
6. Remove the lid and cook for a further 20–25 minutes. Serve immediately.

★ Variation

For a great autumn dish, replace the Mediterranean vegetables with shallots, sage and sliced apple rings.

MEAT

COUNTRY-STYLE HAM WITH PINTO BEANS

Serves: 4 **Prep: 10–15 mins** **Cook: 55 mins**

Ingredients

- 2 tbsp olive oil
- 1 large onion, chopped
- 2 green peppers, deseeded and chopped
- 4 garlic cloves, crushed
- 1 tsp ground cumin
- 500 g/1 lb 2 oz cooked pinto beans
- 3 tbsp tomato ketchup
- 25 g/1 oz molasses sugar or soft dark brown sugar
- 2 tbsp cider vinegar
- 2 tsp gluten-free Worcestershire sauce
- 2 tsp gluten-free French mustard
- 250 g/9 oz cubed cooked ham
- 150 ml/5 fl oz gluten-free vegetable or chicken stock
- salt and pepper (optional)
- chopped fresh flat-leaf parsley, to garnish
- brown rice, to serve

Method

1. Heat the oil in a flameproof casserole set over a medium–low heat, add the onion and peppers and cook for 5 minutes, stirring occasionally. Add the garlic and cumin, stir to combine and cook for a further minute.
2. Stir in the beans, ketchup, sugar, vinegar, Worcestershire sauce, mustard and ham, combining everything well.
3. Add the stock, bring to a simmer, cover with a lid and cook gently for 45 minutes.
4. Season with salt and pepper, if using, and sprinkle over the parsley. Serve with brown rice.

MEAT

BEEF IN BEER WITH HERB DUMPLINGS

Serves: 6 **Prep: 25–30 mins** **Cook: 2 hours 40 mins**

Ingredients

2 tbsp sunflower oil

2 large onions, thinly sliced

8 carrots, sliced

4 tbsp plain flour

1.25 kg/2 lb 12 oz stewing steak, cut into cubes

425 ml/15 fl oz stout

2 tsp muscovado sugar

2 bay leaves

1 tbsp chopped fresh thyme

salt and pepper (optional)

herb dumplings

115 g/4 oz self-raising flour

pinch of salt

55 g/2 oz shredded suet

2 tbsp chopped fresh parsley, plus extra to garnish

about 4 tbsp water

Method

1. Preheat the oven to 160°C/325°F/Gas Mark 3. Heat the oil in a flameproof casserole. Add the onions and carrots and cook over a low heat, stirring occasionally, for 5 minutes, or until the onions are softened. Meanwhile, place the flour in a polythene bag and season to taste, if liked. Add the stewing steak to the bag, tie the top and shake well. Do this in batches, if necessary.

2. Remove the vegetables from the casserole with a slotted spoon and reserve. Add the stewing steak to the casserole, in batches, and cook, stirring frequently, until browned all over.

3. Return the meat and the vegetables to the casserole and sprinkle in any remaining seasoned flour. Pour in the stout and add the sugar, bay leaves and thyme. Bring to the boil, cover and bake in the oven for 1¾ hours.

4. To make the herb dumplings, sift the flour and salt into a bowl. Stir in the suet and parsley and add enough of the water to make a soft dough. Shape into small balls between the palms of your hands. Add to the casserole and return to the oven for 30 minutes.

5. Remove and discard the bay leaves. Serve immediately, sprinkled with chopped parsley.

MEAT

LAMB PILAF

Serves: 4 **Prep: 20 mins** **Cook: 45–50 mins**

Ingredients

2–3 tbsp vegetable oil

650 g/1 lb 7 oz boneless lamb shoulder, cut into 2.5-cm/1-inch cubes

2 onions, roughly chopped

1 tsp ground cumin

200 g/7 oz arborio rice

1 tbsp tomato purée

1 tsp saffron threads

100 ml/3½ fl oz pomegranate juice

850 ml/1½ pints lamb stock, chicken stock or water

115 g/4 oz no-soak dried apricots or prunes, halved

2 tbsp raisins

salt and pepper (optional)

2 tbsp shredded fresh mint

2 tbsp shredded fresh watercress

Method

1. Heat the oil in a large flameproof casserole or saucepan over a high heat. Add the lamb, in batches, and cook over a high heat, turning frequently, for 7 minutes, or until lightly browned.

2. Add the onions, reduce the heat to medium and cook for 2 minutes, or until beginning to soften. Add the cumin and rice and cook, stirring to coat, for 2 minutes, or until the rice is translucent. Stir in the tomato purée and the saffron threads.

3. Add the pomegranate juice and stock. Bring to the boil, stirring. Stir in the apricots and raisins. Reduce the heat to low, cover, and simmer for 20–25 minutes, or until the lamb and rice are tender and all of the liquid has been absorbed.

4. Season to taste with salt and pepper, if using, then sprinkle the shredded mint and watercress over the pilaf and serve straight from the casserole.

MEAT

CHORIZO WITH BARLEY & BUTTER BEANS

Serves: 4 **Prep:** 15 mins **Cook:** 1 hour 20 mins

Ingredients

- 2 tbsp vegetable oil
- 1 onion, chopped
- 3 celery sticks, sliced
- 2 red peppers, deseeded and cut into squares
- 2 tbsp fresh oregano
- 2 large garlic cloves, chopped
- 500 g/1 lb 2 oz chorizo sausage, thickly sliced
- 185 g/6½ oz pearl barley, rinsed
- 1 litre/1¾ pints hot chicken stock
- 400 g/14 oz canned butter beans, drained and rinsed
- salt and pepper (optional)
- green cabbage, to serve (optional)

Method

1. Heat the oil in a flameproof casserole or heavy-based saucepan, add the onion and fry over a medium–high heat for 5 minutes.

2. Add the celery, red peppers, oregano and garlic and fry for a further 5 minutes.

3. Add the chorizo and fry for 5 minutes, turning frequently.

4. Stir in the barley and stock and season to taste with salt and pepper, if using. Bring to the boil, then cover and simmer for about 1 hour, until the barley is tender but still slightly chewy.

5. Add the beans and simmer for 5 minutes to heat through before serving, accompanied by cooked green cabbage, if liked.

MEAT

PORK WITH MIXED GREEN BEANS

Serves: 2 **Prep: 15 mins** **Cook: 10–12 mins**

Ingredients

2 tbsp vegetable or groundnut oil

2 shallots, chopped

225 g/8 oz pork fillet, thinly sliced

2½ cm/1-inch piece fresh galangal or ginger, thinly sliced

2 garlic cloves, chopped

300 ml/10 fl oz chicken stock

4 tbsp chilli sauce

4 tbsp crunchy peanut butter

115 g/4 oz French beans

115 g/4 oz frozen broad beans

115 g/4 oz runner beans, sliced

crispy noodles, to serve

Method

1. Heat the oil in a preheated wok or large frying pan over a high heat.

2. Add the shallots, pork, galangal and garlic and stir-fry for 3–4 minutes until the pork is lightly browned all over.

3. Add the stock, chilli sauce and peanut butter and cook, stirring, until the peanut butter has melted. Add all the beans, stir well and simmer for 3–4 minutes, or until the beans are tender and the pork is cooked through. Serve immediately with crispy noodles.

MEAT

SAUSAGE & BEAN CASSEROLE

Serves: 4 **Prep: 20 mins** **Cook: 25–30 mins**

Ingredients

8 Italian sausages

3 tbsp olive oil

1 large onion, chopped

2 garlic cloves, chopped

1 green pepper, deseeded and sliced

225g/8 oz fresh tomatoes, skinned and chopped or 400 g/14 oz canned chopped tomatoes

2 tbsp sun-dried tomato paste

400 g/14 oz canned cannellini beans, drained

mashed potatoes, to serve

Method

1. Prick the sausages all over with a fork. Heat 2 tablespoons of the oil in a large heavy-based frying pan. Add the sausages and cook over a low heat, turning frequently, for 10–15 minutes, until evenly browned and cooked through. Remove them from the frying pan and keep warm. Drain off the oil and wipe out the pan with kitchen paper.

2. Heat the remaining oil in the frying pan. Add the onion, garlic and green pepper to the frying pan and cook for 5 minutes, stirring occasionally, or until softened.

3. Add the tomatoes to the frying pan and leave the mixture to simmer for about 5 minutes, stirring occasionally, or until slightly reduced and thickened.

4. Stir the sun-dried tomato paste, cannellini beans and sausages into the mixture in the frying pan. Cook for 4–5 minutes, or until the mixture is piping hot. Add 4–5 tablespoons of water if the mixture becomes too dry during cooking.

5. Transfer to serving plates and serve with mashed potatoes.

MEAT

BEEF & VEGETABLE STEW WITH CORN

Serves: 4 **Prep: 20–25 mins** **Cook: 2 hours 25 mins**

Ingredients

450 g/1 lb braising beef steak

1½ tbsp plain flour

1 tsp hot paprika

1–1½ tsp chilli powder

1 tsp ground ginger

2 tbsp olive oil

1 large onion, cut into chunks

3 garlic cloves, sliced

2 celery sticks, sliced

225 g/8 oz carrots, chopped

300 ml/10 fl oz lager

300 ml/10 fl oz beef stock

350 g/12 oz potatoes, chopped

1 red pepper, deseeded and chopped

2 corn on the cob, halved

115 g/4 oz tomatoes, quartered

115 g/4 oz shelled fresh or frozen peas

salt and pepper (optional)

Method

1. Trim any fat or gristle from the beef and cut into 2.5-cm/1-inch chunks. Mix the flour and spices together. Toss the beef in the spiced flour until well coated.

2. Heat the oil in a large, heavy-based saucepan and cook the onion, garlic and celery, stirring frequently, for 5 minutes, or until softened. Add the beef and cook over a high heat, stirring frequently, for 3 minutes, or until browned on all sides and sealed.

3. Add the carrots, then remove from the heat. Gradually stir in the lager and stock, then return to the heat and bring to the boil, stirring. Reduce the heat, cover and simmer, stirring occasionally, for 1½ hours.

4. Add the potatoes to the saucepan and simmer for a further 15 minutes. Add the red pepper and corn on the cob and simmer for a further 15 minutes, then add the tomatoes and peas and simmer for a further 10 minutes, or until the beef and vegetables are tender. Season to taste with salt and pepper, if using.

MEAT

TEXAS LONE-STAR CHILLI

Serves: 4 **Prep: 25 mins** **Cook: 2 hours 20 mins**

Ingredients

2 tbsp vegetable oil

1.3 kg/3 lb stewing steak, cut into 1-cm/½-inch cubes

1 large onion, diced

3 garlic cloves, very finely chopped

2 green bird's eye chillies, deseeded and very finely chopped

2 red jalapeño peppers, deseeded and very finely chopped

2 tbsp hot chilli powder, or to taste

1 tbsp ground cumin

1 tsp dried oregano

1½ tsp salt

½ tsp pepper

¼ tsp cayenne pepper

750 ml/1¼ pints beef stock

280 g/10 oz chopped tomatoes

1 tbsp polenta

water as needed

diced white onion and freshly chopped coriander, to garnish (optional)

Method

1. Heat the oil in a flameproof casserole or large heavy-based pan, and add the beef, in batches if necessary, over a high heat and sear until well browned. Add the onion to the pan, reduce the heat to medium and fry for 5 minutes. Add the garlic and cook for a further 1 minute.

2. Add all the remaining ingredients, except the polenta, and bring to the boil. Reduce the heat to low, cover and simmer for 1 hour, stirring occasionally. Uncover and stir in the polenta. Continue cooking uncovered, stirring occasionally, for a further 1 hour or until the meat is very tender. Add some water during the cooking to adjust the thickness, if necessary, and occasionally skim off any foam that floats to the surface.

3. Taste and adjust the seasoning, if necessary. Serve the chilli immediately, garnished with white onions and coriander, if liked.

MEAT

CINNAMON LAMB CASSEROLE

Serves: 6 **Prep: 20–25 mins** **Cook: 2¼ hours**

Ingredients

- 2 tbsp plain flour
- salt and pepper
- 1 kg/2 lb 4 oz lean boneless lamb, cubed
- 2 tbsp olive oil
- 2 large onions, sliced
- 1 garlic clove, finely chopped
- 300 ml/10 fl oz full-bodied red wine
- 2 tbsp red wine vinegar
- 400 g/14 oz canned chopped tomatoes
- 55 g/2 oz seedless raisins
- 1 tbsp ground cinnamon
- pinch of sugar
- 1 bay leaf
- salt and pepper (optional)
- paprika, to garnish

Topping

- 150 ml/5 fl oz natural Greek yogurt
- 2 garlic cloves, crushed
- salt and pepper (optional)

Method

1. Season the flour with salt and pepper to taste then put it with the lamb in a polythene bag, hold the top closed and shake until the lamb cubes are lightly coated all over. Remove the lamb from the bag, shake off any excess flour and set aside.

2. Heat the oil in a large, flameproof casserole and cook the onions and garlic, stirring frequently, for 5 minutes, or until softened. Add the lamb and cook over a high heat, stirring frequently, for 5 minutes, or until browned on all sides.

3. Stir the wine, vinegar and tomatoes and their juice into the casserole, scraping any sediment from the base of the casserole, and bring to the boil. Reduce the heat and add the raisins, cinnamon, sugar and bay leaf. Season to taste with salt and pepper, if using. Cover and simmer gently for 2 hours, or until the lamb is tender.

4. Meanwhile, make the topping. Put the yogurt into a small serving bowl, stir in the garlic and season to taste with salt and pepper, if using. Cover and chill in the refrigerator until required.

5. Discard the bay leaf and serve hot, topped with a spoonful of the garlicky yogurt and dusted with paprika.

MEAT

FISH & SEAFOOD

MINTED POTATO & HADDOCK ONE POT	108
CREAMY PRAWN PASTA	110
SAFFRON & PRAWN BROTH	112
MIXED SEAFOOD CHOWDER	114
CRAB & VEGETABLE SOUP	116
SALMON & UDON BROTH	118
MISO FISH SOUP	119
GOAN-STYLE SEAFOOD CURRY	120
BAKED SEA BASS	122
UDON NOODLE STIR-FRY WITH FISH CAKE & GINGER	124
PRAWN & CHICKEN PAELLA	126
MUSSELS IN CIDER	128
COCONUT FISH CURRY	129
SQUID & PRAWN STEW	130
MOULES MARINIÈRE	131
SEVEN SEAS SOUP	132
BOUILLABAISSE	134
TUNA NOODLE CASSEROLE	136
COD WITH PINE NUT CRUST & CHERRY TOMATOES	138
FISH STEW WITH CIDER	140
PRAWNS IN MEDITERRANEAN SAUCE	142
SALMON & POTATO CASSEROLE	144
MEDITERRANEAN SWORDFISH	146
MEDITERRANEAN FISH CASSEROLE	147
TUNA CHOWDER	148
SEAFOOD GUMBO	150
MONKFISH RAGOÛT	152
ONE-POT CLAM BAKE	154

MINTED POTATO & HADDOCK ONE POT

Serves: 4 **Prep: 8 mins** **Cook: 30 mins**

Ingredients

- 750 g/1 lb 10 oz new potatoes
- 1 tbsp olive oil
- handful of fresh mint, chopped
- 250 g/9 oz frozen peas, thawed
- 4 spring onions, trimmed and sliced
- 4 haddock fillets, each weighing 150 g/5½ oz
- 2 tbsp snipped fresh chives
- salt and pepper (optional)

Method

1. Preheat the oven to 200°C/400°F/Gas Mark 6.
2. Place the potatoes in a roasting tin with the oil and salt and pepper, if using, and toss to coat. Add the mint and toss again.
3. Roast in the preheated oven for 15 minutes.
4. Stir in the peas and spring onions and lay the haddock fillets on top.
5. Roast for a further 12–15 minutes, until the fish is cooked through and the potatoes are tender.
6. Sprinkle with the chives and serve immediately.

★ Variation

This dish could also be cooked with lamb cutlets added to the roasting tin a bit earlier (depending on how pink you like your lamb).

FISH & SEAFOOD

CREAMY PRAWN PASTA

Serves: 2 **Prep: 15 mins** **Cook: 5 mins**

Ingredients

- 1–2 tsp salt
- 175 g/6 oz dried spaghetti
- 1 tbsp olive oil
- 1 garlic clove, finely sliced
- 100 ml/3½ fl oz white wine
- 2 tbsp crème fraîche
- juice of ½ lemon
- 150 g/5½ oz cooked prawns
- small handful of fresh dill, chopped
- salt and pepper (optional)

Method

1. Add 1–2 teaspoons of salt to a saucepan of water and bring to the boil. Add the pasta, bring back to the boil and cook for 8–10 minutes, or according to the packet instructions. Drain and keep warm.
2. Heat the oil in the pan, add the garlic and cook for 30 seconds, then add the wine and cook over a high heat for 1 minute.
3. Reduce the heat and stir in the crème fraîche and lemon juice. Simmer for 1 minute.
4. Add the prawns and half the dill and season to taste with salt and pepper, if using.
5. Stir the pasta into the sauce and mix well.
6. Serve in two warmed bowls, sprinkled with the remaining chopped dill.

FISH & SEAFOOD

SAFFRON & PRAWN BROTH

Serves: 4   **Prep: 25 mins**   **Cook: 40 mins**

Ingredients

- 200 g/7 oz large raw tiger prawns, heads, tails and shells intact
- 1 kg/2 lb 4 oz fish trimmings, bones and heads
- 1 onion, roughly chopped
- 115 g/4 oz carrots, sliced
- 250 g/9 oz fennel, chopped
- 3 tomatoes, roughly chopped
- pared rind and juice of 1 lemon
- 150 ml/5 fl oz dry white wine
- 1 litre/1¾ pints water
- 2 large pinches of saffron threads
- ½ tsp white peppercorns, roughly crushed
- salt (optional)
- 1 tomato, deseeded and finely diced, to garnish

Method

1. Remove the prawn heads and tails and reserve, then peel away the shell and devein. Chill and reserve the peeled prawns. Add the fish trimmings, bones and heads to a large saucepan with the other prawn trimmings.

2. Add the onion, carrots, fennel, tomatoes and lemon rind to the pan. Pour in the wine and water, then add 1 pinch of the saffron threads and the peppercorns.

3. Bring to the boil, cover and simmer gently for 30 minutes. Strain through a fine sieve into a large measuring jug. You should have about 1.2 litre/ 2 pints. Wipe the pan clean and then pour the strained liquid into the saucepan. If you have too much broth, boil rapidly to reduce it and concentrate the flavours.

4. Add the reserved prawns and the remaining saffron. Cook gently for 2–3 minutes until the prawns are bright pink. Taste the broth and add salt, if using, then add the lemon juice.

5. Ladle the broth into warmed bowls, then garnish with the diced tomato and serve immediately.

FISH & SEAFOOD

MIXED SEAFOOD CHOWDER

Serves: 4 **Prep: 10 mins** **Cook: 30–35 mins**

Ingredients

- 1 tbsp vegetable oil
- 1 large onion, chopped
- 80 g/2¾ oz pancetta, cubed
- 1 tbsp plain flour
- 600 ml/1 pint fish stock, made from 1 fish stock cube
- 225 g/8 oz small new potatoes, halved
- pinch of saffron threads
- pinch of cayenne pepper
- 300 ml/10 fl oz semi-skimmed milk
- 200 g/7 oz haddock or other white fish fillet, cubed
- 150 g/5½ oz salmon fillet, cubed
- 200 g/7 oz cooked shelled mussels
- pepper (optional)

Method

1. Heat the oil in a large saucepan over a medium heat, then add the onion and pancetta. Cook for 8–10 minutes, until the onion is soft and the pancetta is cooked. Stir in the flour and cook for a further 2 minutes.

2. Stir in the stock and bring to a gentle simmer. Add the potatoes, then cover and simmer for 10–12 minutes, until the potatoes are tender and cooked through.

3. Add the saffron, cayenne pepper and pepper, if using, then stir in the milk. Tip the fish into the pan and simmer gently for 4 minutes.

4. Add the mussels and cook for a further 2 minutes to warm through. Serve immediately.

FISH & SEAFOOD

CRAB & VEGETABLE SOUP

Serves: 4 **Prep: 10 mins** **Cook: 25–30 mins**

Ingredients

- 2 tbsp chilli oil
- 1 garlic clove, chopped
- 4 spring onions, trimmed and sliced
- 2 red peppers, deseeded and chopped
- 1 tbsp grated fresh ginger
- 1 litre/1¾ pints fish stock
- 100 ml/3½ fl oz coconut milk
- 100 ml/3½ fl oz rice wine or sherry
- 2 tbsp lime juice
- 1 tbsp grated lime rind
- 6 kaffir lime leaves, finely shredded
- 300 g/10½ oz freshly cooked crabmeat
- 200 g/7 oz freshly cooked crab claws
- 150 g/5½ oz canned sweetcorn, drained
- 1 tbsp chopped fresh coriander
- small handful of fresh coriander, to garnish
- salt and pepper (optional)

Method

1. Heat the oil in a large saucepan over a medium heat. Add the garlic and spring onions and cook, stirring, for about 3 minutes, until slightly softened. Add the red peppers and ginger and cook for a further 4 minutes, stirring.

2. Pour in the stock and season to taste with salt and pepper, if using. Bring to the boil, then reduce the heat. Pour in the coconut milk, rice wine and lime juice, and stir in the grated lime rind and kaffir lime leaves. Simmer for 15 minutes.

3. Add the crabmeat and crab claws to the soup with the sweetcorn and coriander. Cook the soup for 5 minutes until the crab is heated right through.

4. Remove from the heat. Ladle into warmed soup bowls, garnish with coriander and serve immediately.

FISH & SEAFOOD

SALMON & UDON BROTH

Serves: 4 **Prep:** 10 mins **Cook:** 15–20 mins

Ingredients

- 1 litre/1¾ pints vegetable stock
- 2.5-cm/1-inch piece fresh ginger, thinly sliced
- 6 spring onions, finely chopped
- 2 carrots, cut into thin batons
- 2 x 15 g/½ oz miso soup paste
- 250 g/9 oz dried udon noodles
- 250 g/9 oz fresh salmon fillet, cubed
- 125 g/4½ oz shiitake mushrooms, sliced
- 1 fresh red chilli, deseeded and thinly sliced, to garnish
- dark soy sauce (optional)

Method

1. Place the stock in a saucepan with the ginger, spring onions, carrots and miso paste and bring to the boil over a medium–high heat.

2. Meanwhile, cook the noodles in a separate pan of boiling water for 6–8 minutes, or cook according to the packet instructions, until tender. Drain, return to the pan and keep covered until ready to serve.

3. Add the salmon and mushrooms to the broth and cook for 2–3 minutes, until the salmon is cooked through and flakes easily.

4. Divide the cooked noodles between four bowls and top with the salmon broth. Garnish with a little chilli and season to taste with soy sauce, if using.

FISH & SEAFOOD

MISO FISH SOUP

Serves: 4 **Prep: 20 mins** **Cook: 15 mins**

Ingredients

225 g/8 oz sole fillets

850 ml/1½ pints fish stock

2.5-cm/1-inch piece fresh ginger, peeled and grated

1 tbsp nam pla (fish sauce)

1 fresh chilli, deseeded and finely sliced

1 carrot, thinly sliced

½ bunch radishes, trimmed and sliced

1 yellow pepper, deseeded and cut into thin strips

85 g/3 oz shiitake mushrooms, sliced if large

40 g/1½ oz thread egg noodles

1 tbsp miso paste

4 spring onions, trimmed and shredded

Method

1. Skin the sole fillets and cut them into strips.
2. Pour the stock into a large saucepan and add the ginger, nam pla and chilli. Bring to the boil then reduce the heat and simmer for 5 minutes.
3. Add the carrot with the radishes, pepper, mushrooms and noodles and simmer for a further 3 minutes.
4. Add the fish strips with the miso paste and continue to cook for 2 minutes, or until the fish is tender. Divide equally between warmed bowls, top with the spring onions and serve immediately.

FISH & SEAFOOD

GOAN-STYLE SEAFOOD CURRY

Serves: 4–6　　**Prep: 15 mins**　　**Cook: 20 mins**

Ingredients

- 3 tbsp vegetable or groundnut oil
- 1 tbsp black mustard seeds
- 12 fresh curry leaves
- 6 shallots, finely chopped
- 1 garlic clove, crushed
- 1 tsp ground turmeric
- ½ tsp ground coriander
- ¼–½ tsp chilli powder
- 140 g/5 oz creamed coconut, grated and dissolved in 300 ml/10 fl oz boiling water
- 500 g/1 lb 2 oz skinless, boneless white fish, such as monkfish or cod, cut into large chunks
- 450 g/1 lb large raw prawns, peeled and deveined
- juice and finely grated rind of 1 lime
- salt (optional)

Method

1. Heat the oil in a wok or large frying pan over a high heat. Add the mustard seeds and stir them around for about 1 minute, or until they start to pop. Stir in the curry leaves.

2. Add the shallots and garlic and stir-fry for about 5 minutes, or until the shallots are golden. Stir in the turmeric, ground coriander and chilli powder and continue stir-frying for about 30 seconds. Add the dissolved creamed coconut. Bring to the boil, then reduce the heat to medium and stir for about 2 minutes.

3. Reduce the heat to low, add the fish and simmer for 1 minute, spooning the sauce over the fish and very gently stirring it around. Add the prawns and continue to simmer for a further 4–5 minutes, until the fish flakes easily and the prawns curl and turn pink.

4. Add half the lime juice, then taste and add more lime juice and salt, if needed. Sprinkle with the lime rind and serve immediately.

BAKED SEA BASS

Serves: 4 **Prep: 30–35 mins** **Cook: 40–45 mins**

Ingredients

500 g/1 lb 2 oz firm, waxy potatoes, very thinly sliced

1 large garlic clove, very finely chopped

2 onions, thinly sliced

2 tbsp olive oil, plus extra for greasing

2 whole sea bass, haddock, pollack or red snapper, about 400 g/14 oz total weight, heads removed, scaled, gutted and well rinsed

4 fresh thyme sprigs

½ lemon, sliced

150 g/5½ oz black olives, stoned and sliced

salt and pepper

lemon wedges, to serve (optional)

Method

1. Preheat the oven to 220°C/425°F/Gas Mark 7 and grease a roasting dish large enough to hold the fish and potatoes.

2. Arrange the potatoes, garlic and onions in a layer on the bottom of the dish, drizzle over half of the oil and season with salt and pepper, if using. Tightly cover the dish with foil and bake in the preheated oven for 30 minutes, until the potatoes are almost tender.

3. Meanwhile, make three slashes on each side of the fish and rub salt and pepper into the slashes. Divide the thyme sprigs and lemon slices between the fish slashes, then set aside.

4. Reduce the oven temperature to 190°C/375°F/Gas Mark 5. Uncover the dish and stir the olives into the potatoes. Arrange the fish on top, drizzle over the remaining oil, return to the oven and cook for 10 minutes per 2.5 cm/1 inch of fish thickness, or until the fish is cooked through and the flesh flakes easily.

5. Remove the dish from the oven. Fillet and skin the fish and divide the fillets between four warmed plates. Serve with the potatoes, onions and olives, and with lemon wedges for squeezing over, if liked.

FISH & SEAFOOD

UDON NOODLE STIR-FRY WITH FISH CAKE & GINGER

Serves: 2 **Prep: 10 mins** **Cook: 5–10 mins**

Ingredients

2 x 150-g/5½-oz packs ready-to-wok udon noodles

1 leek, shredded

200 g/7 oz beansprouts

8 shiitake mushrooms, finely sliced

2 pieces Japanese fish cake, sliced

12 raw prawns, peeled and deveined

2 eggs, beaten

1 tbsp groundnut or vegetable oil

2 tbsp shoyu (Japanese soy sauce)

3 tbsp mirin

2 tbsp chopped fresh coriander leaves

to serve

chilli oil

2 spring onions, finely sliced

2 tbsp shredded beni-shoga (red ginger)

Method

1. Rinse the noodles under cold running water to remove any oil and tip into a bowl.

2. Add the leek, beansprouts, mushrooms, fish cake, prawns and eggs to the noodles and mix well to combine.

3. Heat a wok over a high heat. Add a little oil and heat until very hot. Add the noodle mixture and stir-fry until golden and the prawns turn pink and start to curl. Add the shoyu, mirin and coriander and toss together.

4. Divide the noodles between two bowls and drizzle with the chilli oil. Sprinkle with the spring onions and beni-shoga and serve immediately.

FISH & SEAFOOD

PRAWN & CHICKEN PAELLA

Serves: 6–8 **Prep: 25–30 mins** **Cook: 40 mins**

Ingredients

- 16 live mussels, scrubbed and debearded
- ½ tsp saffron threads
- 2 tbsp hot water
- 350 g/12 oz paella rice
- 6 tbsp olive oil
- 6–8 unboned chicken thighs, skin-on but with excess fat removed
- 140 g/5 oz Spanish chorizo sausage, casing removed, cut into 5-mm/¼-inch slices
- 2 large onions, chopped
- 4 garlic cloves, crushed
- 1 tsp mild or hot Spanish paprika, to taste
- 100 g/3½ oz green beans, chopped
- 125 g/4½ oz frozen peas
- 1.3 litres/2¼ pints fish, chicken or vegetable stock
- 16 raw prawns, peeled and deveined
- 2 red peppers, halved and deseeded, then grilled, peeled and sliced
- salt and pepper (optional)
- 35 g/1¼ oz fresh chopped parsley, to garnish

Method

1. Discard any mussels with broken shells and any that refuse to close when tapped. Put the saffron and hot water in a bowl and infuse for a few minutes. Meanwhile, put the rice in a sieve and rinse until the water runs clear. Set aside.

2. Heat half the oil in a paella pan or ovenproof casserole. Cook the chicken over medium–high heat, turning frequently, for 5 minutes, or until golden. Transfer to a bowl. Add the chorizo to the pan and cook, stirring, for 1 minute, or until beginning to crisp. Add to the chicken.

3. Heat the remaining oil in the pan and cook the onions, stirring frequently, for 2 minutes. Add the garlic and paprika and cook for 3 minutes.

4. Add the drained rice, beans and peas and stir until coated in oil. Return the chicken and chorizo and any juices to the pan. Stir in the stock, saffron and its soaking liquid, and salt and pepper to taste, if using, and bring to the boil, stirring. Reduce the heat and simmer, uncovered, for 15 minutes, or until the rice is almost tender.

5. Arrange the mussels, prawns and red peppers on top, and cover and simmer, without stirring, until the prawns turn pink and the mussels open. Discard any mussels that remain closed. Sprinkle with parsley and serve.

MUSSELS IN CIDER

Serves: 4 **Prep: 20–25 mins** **Cook: 25 mins**

Ingredients

2 kg/4 lb 8 oz live mussels, scrubbed and debearded

300 ml/10 fl oz dry cider

6 shallots, finely chopped

6 tbsp double cream

pepper (optional)

fresh baguettes, to serve (optional)

Method

1. Discard any mussels with broken shells or any that refuse to close when tapped.

2. Pour the cider into a large casserole, add the shallots and season with pepper, if using. Bring to the boil and cook for 2 minutes.

3. Add the mussels, cover with a tight-fitting lid and cook over a high heat, shaking the casserole dish occasionally, for about 5 minutes, or until the shells have opened. Remove the mussels with a slotted spoon, discarding any that remain closed, and keep warm.

4. Strain the cooking liquid through a muslin-lined sieve into jug, then return the strained liquid to the casserole. Bring to the boil and cook for 8–10 minutes, or until reduced by about half. Stir in the cream and add the mussels. Cook for 1 minute to reheat the shellfish, then serve immediately with fresh baguettes, if liked.

FISH & SEAFOOD

COCONUT FISH CURRY

Serves: 4 **Prep: 10 mins** **Cook: 30–35 mins**

Ingredients

- 2 tsp salt
- 2 tsp ground turmeric
- 4 halibut fillets or steaks, each weighing about 200 g/7 oz
- 2 tbsp vegetable or groundnut oil
- 2 onions, finely sliced
- 4 fresh green chillies, slit lengthways
- 3 garlic cloves, very thinly sliced
- 12 fresh curry leaves
- 400 ml/14 fl oz coconut milk
- 4 tbsp finely chopped fresh coriander

Method

1. Mix a teaspoon of the salt with a teaspoon of the turmeric. Gently rub into the fish fillets and set aside for 10–12 minutes.

2. Meanwhile, heat the oil in a frying pan. Add the onions, chillies and garlic and stir-fry for a few minutes. Add the curry leaves and continue to cook over a low-medium heat for 12–15 minutes, or until the onion is translucent.

3. Add the remaining turmeric and salt to the pan. Pour in the coconut milk and bring to a simmer.

4. Add the fish, in a single layer, and simmer very gently for 5–6 minutes, or until just cooked through.

5. Remove from the heat and scatter over the chopped coriander. Serve immediately.

FISH & SEAFOOD

SQUID & PRAWN STEW

Serves: 4   **Prep: 20 mins**   **Cook: 20–25 mins**

Ingredients

- 2 tbsp olive oil
- 4 spring onions, thinly sliced
- 2 garlic cloves, finely chopped
- 500 g/1 lb 2 oz prepared squid, cut into rings
- 100 ml/3½ fl oz dry white wine
- 600 g/1 lb 5 oz fresh young broad beans in their pods, shelled to give about 225 g/8 oz, or 225 g/8 oz frozen baby broad beans
- 250 g/9 oz raw tiger prawns, peeled and deveined
- 4 tbsp chopped fresh flat-leaf parsley
- salt and pepper (optional)
- crusty bread, to serve

Method

1. Heat the oil in a large frying pan with a lid or a flameproof casserole, add the spring onions and cook over a medium heat, stirring occasionally, for 4–5 minutes, until softened. Add the garlic and cook, stirring, for 30 seconds until softened. Add the squid and cook over a high heat, stirring occasionally, for 2 minutes, or until golden brown.

2. Add the wine and bring to the boil. Add the broad beans, then reduce the heat, cover and simmer for 5–8 minutes if using fresh beans or 4–5 minutes if using frozen beans, until the beans are tender.

3. Add the prawns and parsley, re-cover and simmer for a further 2–3 minutes, until the prawns have turned pink. Season to taste with salt and pepper, if using. Serve immediately with crusty bread to mop up the juices.

FISH & SEAFOOD

MOULES MARINIÈRE

Serves: 4   **Prep: 25 mins**   **Cook: 10 mins**

Ingredients

2 kg/4 lb 8 oz live mussels
300 ml/10 fl oz dry white wine
6 shallots, finely chopped
1 bouquet garni
pepper (optional)
4 bay leaves, to garnish
crusty bread, to serve

Method

1. Clean the mussels by scrubbing or scraping the shells and pulling off any beards. Discard any with broken shells and any that refuse to close when tapped with a knife. Rinse the mussels under cold running water.

2. Pour the wine into a large heavy-based saucepan, add the shallots and bouquet garni and season to taste with pepper, if using. Bring to the boil over a medium heat. Add the mussels, cover tightly and cook, shaking the saucepan occasionally, for 5 minutes.

3. Remove and discard the bouquet garni and any mussels that remain closed. Divide the mussels between 4 soup plates with a slotted spoon. Tilt the casserole to let any sand settle, then spoon the cooking liquid over the mussels. Garnish with bay leaves and serve immediately with fresh crusty bread.

FISH & SEAFOOD

SEVEN SEAS SOUP

Serves: 4 **Prep: 20–25 mins** **Cook: 50 mins**

Ingredients

- 1 tbsp olive oil
- 1 onion, finely chopped
- 2 garlic cloves, finely chopped
- 1 small fennel bulb, green fronds reserved, bulb finely chopped
- 1 red pepper, halved, deseeded and diced
- 500 g/1 lb 2 oz tomatoes, peeled and diced
- 1.2 litres/2 pints vegetable stock
- 55 g/2 oz short-grain brown rice
- ½ tsp dried oregano
- ¼ tsp crushed dried red chillies
- 1 tbsp tomato purée
- 40 g/1½ oz canned dressed brown crabmeat
- 150 g/5½ oz prepared squid, sliced, thawed if frozen
- 225 g/8 oz raw prawns, peeled and deveined and thawed if frozen
- 225 g/8 oz cooked, shelled mussels, thawed if frozen
- 2 tbsp chopped fresh parsley
- grated rind of 1 lemon
- salt and pepper (optional)

Method

1. Heat the oil in a large saucepan, add the onion and fry over a medium heat, stirring, for 5 minutes until soft and just beginning to colour. Stir in the garlic, fennel, red pepper and tomatoes and cook for 3 minutes.

2. Pour in the stock, then add the rice, oregano, chillies and tomato purée. Bring to the boil, stirring, then cover and simmer for 30 minutes until the rice is tender.

3. Stir the crabmeat into the soup, then add the squid, prawns and mussels and cook for 5 minutes until all the prawns are bright pink. Add salt and pepper to taste, if using.

4. Chop the reserved fennel fronds and mix with the parsley and lemon rind. Ladle the soup into warmed shallow bowls, sprinkle the herb mix on top and serve immediately.

FISH & SEAFOOD

BOUILLABAISSE

Serves: 8 **Prep: 25 mins** **Cook: 50–55 mins**

Ingredients

1 kg/2 lb 4 oz selection of at least 4 different firm white fish fillets, such as red mullet, snapper, sea bass, eel or monkfish, scaled and cleaned, but not skinned

100 ml/3½ fl oz olive oil

2 onions, finely chopped

1 fennel bulb, finely chopped

4 garlic cloves, crushed

1.25 kg/2 lb 12 oz canned chopped tomatoes

1.6 litres/2¾ pints fish stock

pinch of saffron strands

grated zest of 1 orange

bouquet garni of 2 thyme sprigs, 2 parsley sprigs and 2 bay leaves, tied together with string

500 g/1 lb 2 oz live mussels, scrubbed and debearded

500 g/1 lb 2 oz cooked prawns, shell on

salt and pepper (optional)

baguette, to serve

Method

1. Carefully pin-bone the fish, then cut the fillets into bite-sized pieces. Heat the olive oil in a very large frying pan or wide saucepan with a lid and gently fry the onion and fennel over a low heat for about 15 minutes, or until soft.

2. Add the garlic and fry for 2 minutes, then add the chopped tomatoes and simmer for 2 minutes.

3. Add the stock, saffron, orange zest and bouquet garni and bring to the boil. Simmer, uncovered, for 15 minutes.

4. Discard any mussels with broken shells and any that refuse to close when tapped. Add the fish pieces, mussels and prawns and cover the pan. Simmer for a further 5–10 minutes, or until the mussels have opened. Discard any that remain closed. Season to taste with salt and pepper, if using, and remove and discard the bouquet garni.

5. Serve immediately in warmed bowls with some baguette, if liked.

FISH & SEAFOOD

TUNA NOODLE CASSEROLE

Serves: 4   **Prep: 15 mins**   **Cook: 30 mins**

Ingredients

1 onion

1 carrot

1 tbsp olive oil

140 g/5 oz button mushrooms

450 ml/16 fl oz chicken stock or vegetable stock

300 ml/10 fl oz canned condensed cream of mushroom soup

475 g/1 lb canned tuna in brine

350 g/12 oz dried egg noodles

125 g/4½ oz panko breadcrumbs

55 g/2 oz freshly grated Parmesan cheese

salt and pepper (optional)

Method

1. Preheat the oven to 200°C/400°F/Gas Mark 6. Dice the onion and carrot. Heat the oil in a large, ovenproof frying pan or wide saucepan. Add the onion and carrot and cook, stirring occasionally. Meanwhile, slice the mushrooms and add them to the pan. Add salt and pepper, if using, and cook, stirring occasionally, for 2–3 minutes, until the vegetables have begun to soften.

2. Stir in the stock and soup and bring to the boil. Drain the tuna and add it to the pan, breaking up any big chunks. Add the noodles and stir to coat with the sauce. Cover the pan and transfer to the preheated oven for about 15 minutes until the noodles are tender.

3. Preheat the grill to medium. Remove the pan from the oven and stir the casserole well. Sprinkle the breadcrumbs and cheese evenly over the top and then place under the grill for 2–3 minutes until the topping is golden brown. Serve immediately.

FISH & SEAFOOD

COD WITH PINE NUT CRUST & CHERRY TOMATOES

Serves: 2 **Prep: 10 mins** **Cook: 15 mins**

Ingredients

- 30 g/1 oz pine nuts
- 15 g/½ oz fresh or dried white breadcrumbs
- grated zest of 1 unwaxed lemon
- 2 tbsp roughly chopped fresh coriander
- pinch of sea salt
- 1 tsp olive oil
- 200 g/7 oz cherry tomatoes on the vine
- 2 cod fillets, about 200 g/7 oz each
- 2 tsp rose harissa

Method

1. Preheat the oven to 200°C/400°F/Gas Mark 6. Crush the pine nuts in a pestle and mortar. Tip them into a bowl, add the breadcrumbs, lemon zest, coriander, salt and oil and mix well.

2. Put the cherry tomatoes on a large baking tray and add the cod fillets skin side-down, arranging everything in a single layer. Spread a teaspoon of rose harissa over each cod fillet, then top with the breadcrumb mixture, pressing down gently.

3. Bake on a high shelf in the oven for 15 minutes, or until the topping is crisp and golden and the fish flakes easily when pressed with a knife. Serve the cod hot with the tomatoes.

FISH & SEAFOOD

FISH STEW WITH CIDER

Serves: 4 **Prep: 25 mins** **Cook: 35 mins**

Ingredients

2 tsp butter
1 large leek, thinly sliced
2 shallots, finely chopped
125 ml/4 fl oz dry cider
300 ml/10 fl oz fish stock
250 g/9 oz potatoes, diced
1 bay leaf
4 tbsp plain flour
200 ml/7 fl oz milk
200 ml/7 fl oz double cream
55 g/2 oz fresh sorrel leaves, chopped
350 g/12 oz skinless monkfish or cod fillet, cut into 2.5-cm/1-inch pieces
salt and pepper (optional)

Method

1. Melt the butter in a large saucepan over a medium-low heat. Add the leek and shallots and cook for about 5 minutes, stirring frequently, until they start to soften. Add the cider and bring to the boil.

2. Stir in the stock, potatoes and bay leaf with some salt, if using (unless the stock is salty), and bring back to the boil. Reduce the heat, cover and cook for a further 10 minutes.

3. Put the flour into a small bowl and very slowly whisk in a few tablespoons of the milk to make a thick paste. Stir in a little more milk to make a smooth liquid.

4. Adjust the heat so the stew bubbles gently. Stir in the flour mixture and cook, stirring frequently, for 5 minutes. Add the remaining milk and half the cream. Continue cooking for about 10 minutes, until the potatoes are tender. Remove and discard the bay leaf.

5. Combine the sorrel with the remaining cream. Stir the sorrel cream into the stew and add the fish. Continue cooking, stirring occasionally, for about 3 minutes, until the monkfish stiffens. Taste the stew and adjust the seasoning, if needed. Ladle into warmed bowls and serve.

FISH & SEAFOOD

PRAWNS IN MEDITERRANEAN SAUCE

Serves: 4

Prep: 20 mins plus cooling and chilling

Cook: 35 mins

Ingredients

- 125 ml/4 fl oz dry white wine
- 125 ml/4 fl oz water
- 6 tbsp olive oil
- 2 large garlic cloves, thinly sliced
- 1 small red onion, finely chopped
- thinly pared zest of 1 large lemon
- 2 tbsp lemon juice
- 1 tbsp coriander seeds, toasted and lightly crushed
- ½ tbsp black or pink peppercorns, lightly crushed
- pinch of dried chilli flakes, or to taste
- 20 raw tiger prawns, peeled and deveined
- salt and pepper (optional)
- chopped fresh flat-leaf parsley, dill or coriander, to garnish
- sliced baguette, to serve

Method

1. Put the wine, water, oil, garlic, onion, lemon zest and juice, coriander seeds, peppercorns and chilli flakes into a saucepan. Cover and bring to the boil over a high heat, then reduce the heat and simmer for 20 minutes.

2. Add the prawns to the liquid and simmer for 2–3 minutes, or until they turn pink. Use a slotted spoon to remove the prawns from the liquid immediately and transfer them to a deep bowl.

3. Bring the poaching liquid back to the boil, uncovered, and boil for 5 minutes, or until reduced by half. Leave to cool to lukewarm, then pour over the prawns. Season the prawns to taste with salt and pepper, if using, and leave to cool completely. Cover the bowl with clingfilm and chill for at least 4 hours.

4. When ready to serve, garnish with parsley and serve chilled, with plenty of sliced baguette for mopping up the juices, if liked.

FISH AND SEAFOOD

SALMON & POTATO CASSEROLE

Serves: 4 **Prep: 25–30 mins** **Cook: 25–30 mins**

Ingredients

- 1 tbsp olive oil, for oiling, plus 2 tbsp olive oil
- 450 g/1 lb new potatoes
- 1 tsp salt
- 350 g/12 oz Brussels sprouts
- ½ tsp pepper
- 675 g/1 lb 8 oz salmon fillet
- 2 tbsp unsalted butter
- 3–4 fresh dill sprigs
- juice of 1 lemon
- 3 spring onions

Method

1. Preheat the oven to 230°C/450°F/Gas Mark 8 and oil a large baking dish. Slice the potatoes into thin rounds and place them in the base of the dish in an even layer. Drizzle half the oil evenly over the potatoes, then sprinkle with half the salt. Place in the preheated oven.

2. Trim and thinly slice the sprouts. Put them into a medium-sized bowl and toss with the remaining oil, half the remaining salt and the pepper. Remove the dish from the oven and spread the sliced sprouts over the top of the potatoes in an even layer. Return to the oven. Cut the salmon into 5-cm/2-inch chunks and season with the remaining salt. Put the butter into a small bowl and melt in the microwave. Finely chop the dill and add it to the butter with the lemon juice. Trim and slice the spring onions.

3. Remove the dish from the oven and place the salmon pieces on top of the vegetables. Spoon the butter mixture over the salmon pieces and drizzle any remaining mixture over the vegetables. Scatter the spring onions over the top. Return to the oven and bake for 10–12 minutes, until the salmon flakes easily with a fork and is cooked through. Serve immediately.

FISH & SEAFOOD

MEDITERRANEAN SWORDFISH

Serves: 4 **Prep: 15–20 mins** **Cook: 45 mins**

Ingredients

2 tbsp olive oil

1 onion, finely chopped

1 celery stick, finely chopped

115 g/4 oz stoned green olives

450 g/1 lb tomatoes, chopped

3 tbsp capers

4 x 140-g/5-oz swordfish steaks

salt and pepper (optional)

fresh flat-leaf parsley sprigs, to garnish

Method

1. Heat the oil in a large, heavy-based frying pan. Add the onion and celery and cook over a low heat, stirring occasionally, for 5 minutes, or until soft.

2. Meanwhile, roughly chop half the olives. Stir the chopped and whole olives into the pan with the tomatoes and capers and season to taste with salt and pepper, if using.

3. Bring to the boil, then reduce the heat, cover and simmer gently, stirring occasionally, for 15 minutes.

4. Add the swordfish steaks to the pan and return to the boil. Reduce the heat, cover and simmer, turning once during cooking, for 20 minutes, until the fish is just cooked through and the flesh flakes easily.

5. Transfer the swordfish steaks to warmed serving plates and spoon the sauce over them. Garnish with the fresh parsley sprigs and serve immediately.

FISH & SEAFOOD

MEDITERRANEAN FISH CASSEROLE

Serves: 6   **Prep: 20–25 mins**   **Cook: 45 mins**

Ingredients

2 tbsp olive oil

1 red onion, sliced and 2 garlic cloves, chopped

2 red peppers, deseeded and thinly sliced

400 g/14 oz canned chopped tomatoes

1 tsp chopped fresh oregano or marjoram

a few saffron strands

450 g/1 lb white fish fillets, cut into chunks

450 g/1 lb prepared squid, cut into rings

300 ml/10 fl oz fish stock

115 g/4 oz cooked prawns

salt and pepper (optional)

2 tbsp chopped fresh parsley, to garnish

Method

1. Peel the cooked prawns. Heat the oil in a frying pan and fry the onion and garlic over a medium heat for 2–3 minutes, until beginning to soften.

2. Add the red peppers to the pan and continue to cook over a low heat for a further 5 minutes. Add the tomatoes, oregano and saffron and stir well.

3. Preheat the oven to 200°C/400°F/Gas Mark 6.

4. Place the fish in a large casserole with the squid. Pour in the vegetable mixture and the stock, stir well and season to taste with salt and pepper, if using.

5. Cover and cook in the preheated oven for about 30 minutes, until the fish is tender and cooked through. Add the prawns and heat through.

6. Spoon into warmed bowls and garnish with the parsley. Serve immediately with crusty bread, if liked, to mop up the casserole juices.

FISH & SEAFOOD

TUNA CHOWDER

Serves: 4 **Prep: 20 mins** **Cook: 50 mins**

Ingredients

- 2 tbsp butter
- 1 large garlic clove, chopped
- 1 large onion, sliced
- 1 carrot, chopped
- 400 g/14 oz potatoes
- 400 g/14 oz canned cannellini beans
- 600 ml/1 pint fish stock
- 400 g/14 oz canned chopped tomatoes
- 1 tbsp tomato purée
- 1 courgette, trimmed and chopped
- 225 g/8 oz canned tuna in brine, drained
- 1 tbsp chopped fresh basil
- 1 tbsp chopped fresh parsley
- 100 ml/3½ fl oz double cream
- salt and pepper (optional)
- fresh basil sprigs, to garnish

Method

1. Melt the butter in a large saucepan over a low heat. Add the garlic and onion and cook, stirring, for 3 minutes, until slightly softened. Add the carrot and cook for a further 5 minutes, stirring.

2. Meanwhile, cut the potatoes into chunks and drain the beans. Pour the stock into the pan, then add the potatoes, beans, tomatoes and tomato purée.

3. Season to taste with salt and pepper, if using. Bring to the boil, then reduce the heat, cover the pan and simmer for 20 minutes.

4. Add the courgette, tuna, chopped basil and parsley and cook for a further 15 minutes. Stir in the cream and cook very gently for a further 2 minutes.

5. Remove from the heat and ladle into warmed bowls. Garnish with sprigs of fresh basil, if liked, and serve immediately.

FISH & SEAFOOD

SEAFOOD GUMBO

Serves: 6 **Prep: 25 mins** **Cook: 35 mins**

Ingredients

2 tbsp sunflower oil

175 g/6 oz okra, trimmed and cut into 2.5-cm/1-inch pieces

2 onions, finely chopped

4 celery sticks, very finely chopped

1 garlic clove, chopped

2 tbsp plain flour

½ tsp caster sugar

1 tsp ground cumin

700 ml/1¼ pints fish stock

1 red pepper and 1 green pepper, deseeded and chopped

2 large tomatoes, chopped

4 tbsp chopped fresh parsley and 1 tbsp chopped fresh coriander

dash of Tabasco sauce

350 g/12 oz cod or haddock fillets, cut into 2.5-cm/1-inch chunks

350 g/12 oz monkfish fillets, cut into 2.5-cm/ 1-inch chunks

350 g/12 oz raw prawns, peeled and deveined

salt and pepper (optional)

Method

1. Heat half the oil in a large flameproof casserole or a large saucepan with a tight-fitting lid and cook the okra over a low heat, stirring frequently, for 5 minutes, or until browned. Using a slotted spoon, remove from the casserole and set aside.

2. Heat the remaining oil in the casserole and cook the onion and celery over a medium heat, stirring frequently, for 5 minutes, or until softened. Add the garlic and cook, stirring, for 1 minute. Sprinkle in the flour, sugar and cumin with salt and pepper to taste, if using. Cook, stirring constantly, for 2 minutes, then remove from the heat.

3. Gradually stir in the stock, then return to the heat and bring to the boil, stirring. Return the okra to the casserole and add the peppers and tomatoes. Partially cover, reduce the heat to very low and simmer gently, stirring occasionally, for 10 minutes.

4. Add the herbs and Tabasco sauce to taste. Gently stir in the fish and prawns. Cover and simmer gently for 5 minutes, or until the fish is cooked through and the prawns have turned pink. Transfer to a warmed serving dish and serve immediately.

FISH & SEAFOOD

MONKFISH RAGOÛT

Serves: 4–6 **Prep: 25 mins** **Cook: 35 mins**

Ingredients

- 2 tbsp olive oil
- 1 small onion, finely chopped
- 1 red pepper, deseeded and cut into 2.5-cm/1-inch pieces
- 115 g/4 oz mushrooms, finely sliced
- 3 garlic cloves, very finely chopped
- 1 tbsp tomato purée
- 2 tbsp chopped fresh flat-leaf parsley
- ½ tsp dried oregano
- 400 g/14 oz canned chopped tomatoes
- 150 ml/5 fl oz dry red wine
- 550 g/1 lb 4 oz monkfish fillets, cut into chunks
- 1 courgette, sliced
- salt and pepper (optional)
- 6–8 fresh basil leaves, shredded, to garnish
- crusty bread, to serve

Method

1. Heat the oil in a heavy-based saucepan or flameproof casserole over a medium heat. Add the onion, red pepper and mushrooms and cook for 5 minutes, or until beginning to soften.

2. Stir in the garlic, tomato purée, parsley and oregano. Cook for 1 minute. Pour in the tomatoes and wine. Season to taste with salt and pepper, if using. Bring to the boil, then reduce the heat and simmer gently for 10–15 minutes, or until slightly thickened.

3. Add the monkfish and courgette. Cover and simmer for 15 minutes, or until the monkfish is cooked through and the courgette is tender but still brightly coloured.

4. Garnish with the basil and serve immediately with crusty bread.

★ Variation

You can replace the monkfish with another firm-fleshed fish, such as cod, swordfish, halibut or sea bass.

FISH & SEAFOOD

ONE-POT CLAM BAKE

Serves: 4 **Prep: 25–30 mins** **Cook: 35–40 mins, plus standing**

Ingredients

- 2 tbsp olive oil
- 25 g/1 oz butter
- 4 shallots, finely chopped
- 4 garlic cloves, chopped
- 4 celery sticks, finely chopped
- 1 tbsp smoked paprika
- 475 ml/17 fl oz apple cider
- 2 litres/3½ pints chicken stock
- 500 g/1 lb 2 oz new potatoes
- 2 corn cobs, each cut into 3
- 200 g/7 oz smoked sausage, sliced
- 1 kg/2 lb 4 oz live clams, scrubbed
- 1 kg/2 lb 4 oz large raw prawns, shells on
- small bunch fresh parsley, chopped
- salt and pepper (optional)
- crusty bread, to serve

Method

1. Add the olive oil, butter, shallots, garlic and celery to a large casserole with a tight-fitting lid. Cook uncovered over a medium–low heat for 10 minutes, or until the shallots are translucent.

2. Add the smoked paprika, cider and hot chicken stock, bring to the boil and add the new potatoes. Cover and simmer for 10 minutes, then add the corn cobs and smoked sausage. Cook for a further 10 minutes, until the potatoes are almost soft.

3. Discard any clams with broken shells and any that refuse to close when tapped. Add the clams and prawns to the casserole, and cook for a further 2 minutes, until the clams have opened and the prawns have turned pink. Discard any clams that remain closed.

4. Remove from the heat and leave for a couple of minutes, then add the chopped parsley and season with salt and pepper to taste, if using. Transfer to a large serving dish and serve immediately with crusty bread, if liked.

FISH & SEAFOOD

VEGETABLES

SWEET POTATO & APPLE SOUP	158
WARM VEGETABLE MEDLEY	160
BROWN RICE RISOTTO PRIMAVERA	162
MINESTRONE SOUP	164
MEXICAN QUINOA CHILLI	166
BUTTERNUT SQUASH & LENTIL STEW	168
YOGURT, POMEGRANATE & PEANUT RAITA	169
SPANISH VEGETABLE STEW	170
TANDOORI MUSHROOM CURRY	172
VEGETABLE STEW WITH COUSCOUS	174
POTATO & MUSHROOM PIE	176
TOFU PARCELS	178
CELERIAC & NEW POTATO SMASH	179
CABBAGE & WALNUT STIR-FRY	180
POTATO & LEMON CASSEROLE	181
PESTO POTATOES & BEANS	182
EGG-FRIED RICE WITH VEGETABLES	184
ONION & ROOT VEGETABLE WINTER ROAST	186
KALE, SWEET POTATO & PEANUT STEW	188
SPICY VEGETABLE STEW	190
CAULIFLOWER AND SWEET POTATO CURRY	192
SHAKSHOUKA	194
BRAISED PEAS WITH LETTUCE & TARRAGON	196
AUBERGINE GRATIN	197
VEGETABLE PHO	198
PERSIAN HERB FRITTATA	200
HOT & SOUR NOODLES WITH TOFU	202
SQUASH, KALE & FARRO STEW	204

SWEET POTATO & APPLE SOUP

Serves: 6 **Prep: 20 mins** **Cook: 50 mins**

Ingredients

- 1 tbsp butter
- 3 leeks, thinly sliced
- 1 large carrot, thinly sliced
- 600 g/1 lb 5 oz sweet potatoes, diced
- 2 large Bramley apples, peeled, cored and diced
- 1.2 litres/2 pints water
- ¼ tsp freshly grated nutmeg, or to taste
- 225 ml/8 fl oz apple juice
- 225 ml/8 fl oz single cream
- salt and pepper (optional)
- 2 tbsp snipped fresh chives or coriander, to garnish

Method

1. Melt the butter in a large saucepan over a medium-low heat.
2. Add the leeks, cover and cook for 6–8 minutes, or until soft, stirring frequently.
3. Add the carrot, sweet potatoes, apples and water. Lightly season to taste with salt and pepper, if using, and add the nutmeg. Bring to the boil, reduce the heat and simmer, covered, for about 20 minutes, stirring occasionally, until the vegetables are very tender.
4. Leave the soup to cool slightly, then purée in the pan with a hand-held blender.
5. Stir in the apple juice, place over a low heat and simmer for about 10 minutes, until heated through.
6. Stir in the cream and simmer for a further 5 minutes, stirring frequently, until heated through. Taste and adjust the seasoning, if necessary.
7. Ladle the soup into warmed bowls, garnish with chives and serve immediately.

VEGETABLES

WARM VEGETABLE MEDLEY

Serves: 4 **Prep: 20 mins** plus cooling **Cook: 22 mins**

Ingredients

4 tbsp olive oil
2 celery sticks, sliced
2 red onions, sliced
450 g/1 lb aubergines, diced
1 garlic clove, finely chopped
5 plum tomatoes, chopped
3 tbsp red wine vinegar
1 tbsp sugar
3 tbsp stoned green olives
2 tbsp drained capers
salt and pepper (optional)
4 tbsp chopped fresh flat-leaf parsley, to garnish
fresh ciabatta bread, to serve

Method

1. Heat half the oil in a large, heavy-based saucepan. Add the celery and onions and cook over a low heat, stirring occasionally, for 5 minutes, until soft but not coloured. Add the remaining oil and the aubergines. Cook, stirring frequently, for about 5 minutes, until the aubergines begin to colour.

2. Add the garlic, tomatoes, vinegar and sugar and mix well. Cover the mixture with a round of greaseproof paper and simmer gently for about 10 minutes.

3. Remove and discard the greaseproof paper, then stir in the olives and capers. Season to taste with salt and pepper, if using.

4. Tip the mixture into a serving dish and leave to cool slightly. Garnish with the parsley and serve with fresh ciabatta.

VEGETABLES

BROWN RICE RISOTTO PRIMAVERA

Serves: 4 **Prep: 25 mins** **Cook: 45 mins**

Ingredients

- 1.2 litres/2 pints vegetable stock
- 1 tbsp olive oil
- 1 large leek, thinly sliced, white and green slices kept separate
- 2 garlic cloves, finely chopped
- 250 g/9 oz short-grain brown rice
- 150 g/5½ oz baby carrots, tops trimmed, halved lengthways
- 100 g/3½ oz asparagus spears, woody stems removed
- 225 g/8 oz courgettes, cut into cubes
- 25 g/1 oz butter
- 70 g/2½ oz Parmesan cheese, finely grated
- 60 g/2¼ oz mixed baby spinach, watercress and rocket leaves

Method

1. Bring the stock to the boil in a saucepan.
2. Meanwhile, heat the oil in a large frying pan over a medium heat. Add the white leek slices and garlic and cook for 3–4 minutes, or until softened but not browned.
3. Stir the rice into the pan and cook for 1 minute. Pour in half of the hot stock, bring back to the boil, then cover and simmer for 15 minutes.
4. Add the carrots and half of the remaining stock and stir again. Cover and cook for 15 minutes.
5. Add the green leek slices, asparagus and courgettes to the rice, then add a little extra stock. Re-cover and cook for 5–6 minutes, or until the vegetables and rice are just tender.
6. Remove from the heat, stir in the butter and two-thirds of the cheese, and add a little more stock if needed. Top with the mixed leaves, cover with the lid, and warm through for 1–2 minutes, or until the leaves are just beginning to wilt.
7. Spoon the risotto into warmed shallow bowls, sprinkle with the remaining cheese and serve immediately.

VEGETABLES

MINESTRONE SOUP

Serves: 4 **Prep: 20–25 mins** **Cook: 50 mins**

Ingredients

- 2 tbsp olive oil
- 2 garlic cloves, chopped
- 2 red onions, chopped
- 75 g/2¾ oz Parma ham, sliced
- 1 red pepper and 1 orange pepper
- 400 g/14 oz canned chopped tomatoes
- 1 litre/1¾ pints vegetable stock
- 1 celery stick, chopped
- 400 g/14 oz canned borlotti beans
- 100 g/3½ oz leafy green cabbage
- 75 g/2¾ oz frozen peas
- 1 tbsp chopped fresh parsley
- 75 g/2¾ oz dried vermicelli pasta
- salt and pepper (optional)
- freshly grated Parmesan cheese, to serve

Method

1. Heat the oil in a large saucepan. Add the garlic, onions and ham and cook over a medium heat, stirring, for 3 minutes, until slightly softened.

2. Deseed and chop the red pepper and orange pepper, add to the pan with the chopped tomatoes and cook for a further 2 minutes, stirring. Stir in the stock, then add the celery.

3. Drain and rinse the beans and shred the cabbage, then add to the pan with the peas and parsley. Season to taste with salt and pepper, if using. Bring to the boil, then reduce the heat and simmer for 30 minutes.

4. Add the pasta to the pan. Cook for a further 8–10 minutes, then remove from the heat and ladle into warmed bowls. Sprinkle with Parmesan cheese and serve.

VEGETABLES

MEXICAN QUINOA CHILLI

Serves: 4 **Prep: 15 mins** **Cook: 30–35 mins**

Ingredients

1 tbsp olive oil
1 red onion, diced
1 carrot, diced
1 celery stick, diced
1 red chilli, deseeded and finely diced
2 garlic cloves, diced
1 tsp paprika
1 tsp chilli powder
250 g/9 oz fresh beef mince
75 g/2¾ oz quinoa
200 ml/7 fl oz beef stock
400 g/14 oz canned chopped tomatoes
1 tbsp tomato purée
400 g/14 oz canned kidney beans, drained
400 g/14 oz canned cannellini beans, drained
salt and pepper (optional)
handful of fresh coriander leaves, to garnish

Method

1. Heat the oil in a large frying pan, add the onion, carrot and celery and sauté for 2–3 minutes.

2. Stir in the chilli and garlic and cook for 1 minute, then stir in the paprika and chilli powder and cook for a further minute.

3. Add the mince and cook, breaking it up with a wooden spoon, for 2–3 minutes, until brown all over. Stir in the quinoa and cook for 1 minute.

4. Pour in the stock and chopped tomatoes, then stir in the tomato purée.

5. Add the kidney beans and cannellini beans, stirring to combine, then bring to the boil and simmer for 20–25 minutes, until most of the liquid has been absorbed. Season to taste with salt and pepper, if using

6. Serve in warmed bowls, sprinkled with the coriander leaves.

★ **Variation**

If you want to serve this as a vegetarian chilli, omit the beef and increase the quantity of beans and quinoa by half.

VEGETABLES

BUTTERNUT SQUASH & LENTIL STEW

Serves: 4 **Prep: 15–20 mins** **Cook: 35 mins**

Ingredients

- 1 tbsp olive oil
- 1 onion, finely chopped
- 3 garlic cloves, chopped
- 2 level tbsp tomato purée
- 2 tsp ground cumin
- 1 tsp ground cinnamon
- ¼ tsp cayenne pepper
- 450 g/1 lb butternut squash flesh, cut into cubes
- 100 g/3½ oz brown lentils
- 450 ml/16 fl oz vegetable stock
- juice of ¼ lemon
- sea salt and pepper (optional)
- finely chopped fresh coriander, flaked almonds and natural yogurt, to serve

Method

1. Heat the oil in a large saucepan over a medium-high heat. Add the onion and garlic and cook, stirring occasionally, for 5 minutes, or until soft.

2. Add the tomato purée, cumin, cinnamon and cayenne and season well with salt and pepper, if using, and then stir. Add the squash, lentils and stock, and bring to the boil. Reduce the heat to low and simmer uncovered, stirring occasionally, for 25 minutes, or until the squash and lentils are tender.

3. Just before serving, stir in the lemon juice. Serve hot, sprinkled with the coriander and almonds, with a spoonful of yogurt on top.

VEGETABLES

YOGURT, POMEGRANATE & PEANUT RAITA

Serves: 4 **Prep: 10 mins** **Cook: 4–5 mins**

Ingredients

- 2 tbsp vegetable oil
- 4 shallots, finely chopped
- 2 fresh green chillies, finely chopped
- 2 tsp grated fresh ginger
- 1 tsp black mustard seeds
- 4 fresh curry leaves
- 2 whole dried red chillies, broken in half
- 2 tsp cumin seeds
- 225 g/8 oz natural yogurt, whisked
- 1 tsp salt
- 4 tbsp grated coconut
- 2 tbsp finely chopped fresh coriander
- 2 tbsp pomegranate seeds
- 2 tbsp roughly chopped toasted peanuts

Method

1. Heat the oil in a frying pan, add the shallots and stir-fry over a low heat for 3–4 minutes.
2. Add the green chillies, ginger, mustard seeds, curry leaves, dried red chillies and cumin seeds. Stir-fry for 1 minute, then remove from the heat.
3. Stir in the yogurt, salt, coconut and coriander. Stir to mix well and transfer to a serving bowl. Scatter over the pomegranate seeds and peanuts just before serving.

VEGETABLES

SPANISH VEGETABLE STEW

Serves: 4 **Prep: 25 mins** **Cook: 55 mins**

Ingredients

- 2 tbsp virgin olive oil
- 1 onion, roughly chopped
- 1 aubergine, roughly chopped
- ½ tsp smoked hot paprika
- 2 garlic cloves, finely chopped
- 1 large red pepper, deseeded and roughly chopped
- 250 g/9 oz baby new potatoes, unpeeled and any larger ones halved
- 450 g/1 lb plum tomatoes, peeled and roughly chopped
- 400 g/14 oz canned haricot beans in water, drained and rinsed
- 150 ml/5 fl oz vegetable stock
- 2 sprigs of fresh rosemary
- 2 courgettes, roughly chopped
- salt and pepper (optional)

Method

1. Preheat the oven to 200°C/400°F/Gas Mark 6. Heat 1 tablespoon of oil in a saucepan over a medium heat. Add the onion and fry for 5 minutes, or until softened. Add another tablespoon of oil, then add the aubergine, and fry, stirring, for 5 minutes, or until just beginning to soften and brown.

2. Stir in the smoked paprika and garlic, then the red pepper, potatoes and tomatoes. Add the haricot beans, stock and rosemary, then season with salt and pepper, if using. Bring to the boil, cover, turn the heat down to medium–low and simmer for 30 minutes, stirring from time to time.

3. Stir the courgettes into the stew, then cook, uncovered, for 10 minutes, or until all the vegetables are tender and the sauce has reduced slightly.

4. Ladle the stew into warmed shallow bowls, discard the rosemary sprigs and serve immediately.

VEGETABLES

TANDOORI MUSHROOM CURRY

Serves: 4 **Prep: 15–20 mins** **Cook: 35 mins**

Ingredients

- 2 tbsp vegetable or groundnut oil
- 1 tsp cumin seeds
- 1 tsp coriander seeds
- 1 onion, finely chopped
- 2 tsp ground coriander
- 1 tsp ground cumin
- 6 black peppercorns
- ½ tsp freshly ground cardamom seeds
- 1 tsp ground turmeric
- 1 tbsp tandoori masala powder
- 1 fresh red chilli, finely chopped
- 2 garlic cloves, crushed
- 2 tsp grated fresh ginger
- 800 g/1 lb 12 oz canned chopped tomatoes
- 600 g/1 lb 5 oz chestnut or button mushrooms, halved or thickly sliced
- 2 tsp salt
- 200 g/7 oz fresh or frozen peas
- 4 tbsp roughly chopped fresh coriander
- 6 tbsp single cream

Method

1. Heat the oil in a large saucepan over a medium heat. Add the cumin seeds and coriander seeds and cook for 1 minute, or until sizzling.

2. Add the onion, ground coriander, ground cumin, peppercorns, ground cardamom seeds, turmeric, tandoori masala powder, chilli, garlic and ginger. Cook, stirring, for 2–3 minutes, or until the onion is soft and the mixture is aromatic.

3. Add the tomatoes, mushrooms and salt and stir until well combined. Bring to the boil, then reduce the heat to low and cook, uncovered, for 25 minutes.

4. Add the peas and stir to mix well. Cook for a further 4–5 minutes, or until piping hot.

5. Remove from the heat, scatter over the fresh coriander and drizzle over the cream. Stir to mix well. Serve immediately.

VEGETABLES

VEGETABLE STEW WITH COUSCOUS

Serves: 4 **Prep: 20 mins** **Cook: 15 mins, plus 5 mins standing**

Ingredients

1 onion
2 garlic cloves
2 tbsp olive oil
1 orange or red pepper
225 g/8 oz French beans
400 g/14 oz canned chickpeas
2 tbsp garam masala
1 tsp salt
225 ml/8 fl oz vegetable stock
400 g/14 oz canned chopped tomatoes with their can juices
200 g/7 oz couscous
300 g/10½ oz washed baby spinach
juice of 1 lemon
2 tbsp chopped fresh parsley
natural yogurt, sriracha sauce and chia seeds, to garnish (optional)

Method

1. Dice the onion and finely chop the garlic. Heat the oil in a large frying pan over a medium-high heat. Add the onion and garlic and cook, stirring occasionally, for about 5 minutes, until the onion is soft. Meanwhile, deseed and dice the orange pepper. Top and tail the beans and cut them into 5-cm/2-inch pieces. Drain and rinse the chickpeas.

2. Add the beans and orange pepper to the pan with the chickpeas, garam masala and salt. Add the stock and the tomatoes with their can juices and bring to the boil. Cook for about 4 minutes, until the beans begin to soften. Stir in the couscous and spinach, remove from the heat and cover. Leave to stand for about 5 minutes, until the couscous is tender and the spinach is wilted.

3. Stir the lemon juice into the stew with the parsley. Serve hot.

VEGETABLES

POTATO & MUSHROOM PIE

Serves: 4 **Prep: 20–25 mins** **Cook: 50 mins**

Ingredients

- 2 tbsp butter
- 500 g/1 lb 2 oz waxy potatoes, thinly sliced and parboiled
- 150 g/5½ oz sliced mixed mushrooms
- 1 tbsp chopped fresh rosemary
- 4 tbsp snipped chives, plus extra to garnish
- 2 garlic cloves, crushed
- 150 ml/5 fl oz double cream
- salt and pepper (optional)

Method

1. Preheat the oven to 190°C/375°F/Gas Mark 5. Grease a shallow ovenproof dish with the butter.
2. Layer a quarter of the potatoes in the base of the dish. Arrange one third of the mushrooms on top of the potatoes and sprinkle with one third of the rosemary, chives and garlic. Continue making the layers in the same order, and finish with a layer of potatoes on top.
3. Pour the double cream evenly over the top of the potatoes. Season to taste with salt and pepper, if using.
4. Place the dish in the preheated oven, and cook for about 45 minutes, or until the pie is golden brown and piping hot.
5. Garnish with snipped chives and serve immediately, straight from the dish.

VEGETABLES

TOFU PARCELS

Serves: 4 **Prep: 10 mins** **Cook: 10–15 mins**

Ingredients

2 tbsp olive oil

1 garlic clove, crushed

250 g/9 oz firm tofu, cut into chunks

250 g/9 oz cherry tomatoes, halved

1 small red onion, thinly sliced

handful of fresh basil leaves

salt and pepper (optional)

Method

1. Preheat the oven to 220°C/425°F/Gas Mark 7. Brush four 30-cm/12-inch squares of double-thickness foil with oil. Mix the remaining oil with the garlic.

2. Divide the tofu, tomatoes, onion and basil between the foil squares, sprinkle with salt and pepper, if using, and spoon over the garlic-flavoured oil.

3. Fold over the foil to enclose the filling and seal firmly. Place on a baking sheet in the preheated oven and cook for 10–15 minutes, until heated through.

4. Carefully open the parcels and serve.

VEGETABLES

CELERIAC & NEW POTATO SMASH

Serves: 4 **Prep: 15 mins** **Cook: 25 mins**

Ingredients

- 1 small celeriac, peeled and cut into 2-cm/¾-inch chunks
- 400 g/14 oz new potatoes, scrubbed and cut into 2-cm/¾-inch chunks
- 2 garlic cloves, crushed
- 1 tbsp olive oil
- 100 ml/3½ fl oz vegetable stock
- ½ tsp celery salt
- 2 tsp fresh thyme leaves
- 1 tbsp chopped fresh flat-leaf parsley
- pepper (optional)

Method

1. Put the celeriac into a large frying pan over a medium-high heat. Add the potatoes, garlic and oil and stir. Fry for 3–4 minutes, stirring occasionally, until the vegetables are lightly coloured.

2. Pour in the stock, add the celery salt, thyme, and pepper, if using, and bring to a simmer. Cover and braise the vegetables for 20 minutes, adding a little water if they begin to look dry.

3. Using a potato masher, bash the vegetables in the pan – don't mash them, just break them down into smallish pieces. Sprinkle over the parsley, stir and serve immediately.

VEGETABLES

CABBAGE & WALNUT STIR-FRY

Serves: 4 **Prep: 20 mins** **Cook: 15 mins**

Ingredients

4 tbsp groundnut oil

1 tbsp walnut oil

2 garlic cloves, crushed

350 g/12 oz white cabbage, thinly shredded

350 g/12 oz red cabbage, thinly shredded

8 spring onions, trimmed

225 g/8 oz firm tofu, cubed

2 tbsp lemon juice

100 g/3½ oz walnut halves

2 tsp Dijon mustard

salt and pepper (optional)

2 tsp poppy seeds, to garnish

Method

1. Heat the groundnut oil and walnut oil in a preheated wok. Add the garlic, white cabbage, red cabbage, spring onions and tofu and cook for 5 minutes, stirring.

2. Add the lemon juice, walnuts and mustard to the wok and stir to combine thoroughly.

3. Season the mixture with salt and pepper, if using, and cook for a further 5 minutes, or until the cabbage is tender.

4. Transfer the stir-fry to a warmed serving bowl, garnish with the poppy seeds and serve immediately.

VEGETABLES

POTATO & LEMON CASSEROLE

Serves: 4 **Prep: 20 mins** **Cook: 30–40 mins**

Ingredients

- 100 ml/3½ fl oz olive oil
- 2 red onions, cut into 8 wedges
- 3 garlic cloves, crushed
- 2 tsp ground cumin
- 2 tsp ground coriander
- pinch of cayenne pepper
- 1 carrot, thickly sliced
- 2 small turnips, quartered
- 1 courgette, sliced
- 500 g/1 lb 2 oz potatoes, thickly sliced
- juice and grated rind of 2 large lemons
- 300 ml/10 fl oz vegetable stock
- 2 tbsp chopped fresh coriander
- salt and pepper (optional)

Method

1. Heat the oil in a flameproof casserole. Add the onions and sauté over a medium heat, stirring frequently, for 3 minutes.
2. Add the garlic and cook for 30 seconds. Stir in the ground cumin, ground coriander and cayenne pepper and cook, stirring constantly, for 1 minute.
3. Add the carrot, turnips, courgette and potatoes and stir to coat in the oil.
4. Add the lemon juice and rind and the stock. Season to taste with salt and pepper, if using. Cover and cook over a medium heat, stirring occasionally, for 20–30 minutes until tender.
5. Remove the lid, sprinkle in the chopped fresh coriander and stir well. Serve immediately.

VEGETABLES

PESTO POTATOES & BEANS

Serves: 4 **Prep: 10 mins** **Cook: 35–40 mins**

Ingredients

- 750 g/1 lb 10 oz new potatoes, cut into large bite-sized pieces
- 150 g/5½ oz broad beans
- 2 tbsp pesto
- 3 back bacon rashers, chopped
- 3 tbsp fresh Parmesan cheese shavings
- 12 fresh basil leaves, torn

Method

1. Preheat the oven to 200°C/400°F/Gas Mark 6.
2. Place a large piece of foil in a roasting tin and place the potatoes and broad beans in the centre.
3. Sprinkle over the pesto and gently toss. Sprinkle over the bacon bits and bring up the edges of the foil to seal completely.
4. Roast in the preheated oven for 35–40 minutes, until the potatoes are tender.
5. Sprinkle with the cheese shavings and basil leaves and serve immediately.

VEGETABLES

EGG-FRIED RICE WITH VEGETABLES

Serves: 4　　　**Prep: 20 mins**　　　**Cook: 17–20 mins**

Ingredients

2 tbsp vegetable or groundnut oil

2 garlic cloves, finely chopped

2 fresh red chillies, deseeded and chopped

115 g/4 oz mushrooms, sliced

50 g/2 oz mangetout, halved

50 g/2 oz baby sweetcorn, halved

3 tbsp Thai soy sauce

1 tbsp palm sugar or soft, light brown sugar

a few Thai basil leaves

350 g/12 oz rice, cooked and cooled

2 eggs, beaten

crispy onion topping (optional)

2 tbsp vegetable or groundnut oil

2 onions, sliced

Method

1. Heat the oil in a wok or large frying pan and fry the garlic and chillies for 2–3 minutes.

2. Add the mushrooms, mangetout and baby sweetcorn and stir-fry for 2–3 minutes before adding the soy sauce, sugar and basil. Stir in the rice.

3. Push the mixture to one side of the wok. Add the eggs to the wok and stir until lightly set before combining with the rice mixture.

4. If you wish to make the optional crispy onion topping, heat the oil in another frying pan and sauté the onions until crispy and brown. Serve the rice topped with the onions.

VEGETABLES

ONION & ROOT VEGETABLE WINTER ROAST

Serves: 4 **Prep: 15 mins** **Cook: 45 mins**

Ingredients

2 red onions, quartered, about 200 g/7 oz total weight

6 small shallots

200 g/7 oz parsnips, cut into thick batons

200 g/7 oz sweet potatoes, cut into thick batons

200 g/7 oz yams, cut into thick batons

150 g/5½ oz Jerusalem artichokes, scrubbed and halved

8 large garlic cloves, unpeeled

1 tbsp rapeseed oil

1 tbsp lemon juice

1 tsp salt

pepper (optional)

Method

1. Preheat the oven to 190°C/375°F/Gas Mark 5. Place the onions and shallots in a roasting tin.

2. Add the parsnips, sweet potatoes, yams, Jerusalem artichokes and garlic to the roasting tin.

3. Pour in the oil and lemon juice. Add the salt and pepper to taste, if using, then stir so that the vegetables are thoroughly coated with the oil and lemon juice.

4. Bake in the preheated oven for 20 minutes. Turn the vegetables with a spatula and bake for a further 25 minutes, or until they are golden and cooked through. The garlic cloves should be meltingly soft inside – if you like, press the contents of each garlic clove out and into the pan juices and stir in with a little water. Serve immediately.

VEGETABLES

KALE, SWEET POTATO & PEANUT STEW

Serves: 4 **Prep: 15–20 mins** **Cook: 35–40 mins**

Ingredients

- 2 tbsp olive oil
- 1 large onion, sliced
- 1 garlic clove, crushed
- 2 tsp ground coriander
- 1 tsp ground cumin
- 400 g/14 oz sweet potatoes, cut into 2-cm/¾-inch chunks
- 400 g/14 oz canned chopped tomatoes
- 2 bay leaves
- 300 ml/10 fl oz vegetable stock
- 140 g/5 oz crunchy peanut butter
- 200 g/7 oz curly kale, thickly sliced
- salt and pepper (optional)
- 55 g/2 oz salted peanuts, lightly toasted, to garnish
- fresh crusty bread, to serve

Method

1. Heat the oil in a large saucepan over a medium heat, add the onion and fry, stirring occasionally, for about 5 minutes, until soft but not brown. Stir in the garlic, coriander and cumin and gently fry, stirring, for about 30 seconds.

2. Stir in the sweet potatoes, tomatoes, bay leaves and stock and bring to the boil. Reduce the heat to low, cover with a lid and simmer gently for 15–20 minutes, until the potatoes are tender.

3. Stir in the peanut butter and season to taste with salt and pepper, if using. Stir in the kale, cover and simmer for a further 5–6 minutes, stirring occasionally, until just tender.

4. Spoon into a serving dish and scatter with toasted peanuts. Serve hot, with fresh crusty bread.

VEGETABLES

SPICY VEGETABLE STEW

Serves: 4 **Prep: 30 mins** **Cook: 1 hour 25 mins–1½ hours**

Ingredients

- 1 aubergine, cut into 2.5-cm/1-inch slices
- 1 tbsp olive oil, plus extra for brushing
- 1 large red or yellow onion, finely chopped
- 2 red or yellow peppers, deseeded and finely chopped
- 3–4 garlic cloves, finely chopped or crushed
- 800 g/1 lb 12 oz canned chopped tomatoes
- 1 tbsp mild chilli powder
- ½ tsp ground cumin
- ½ tsp dried oregano
- 2 small courgettes, quartered lengthways and sliced
- 400 g/14 oz canned kidney beans, drained and rinsed
- 450 ml/16 fl oz water
- 1 tbsp tomato purée
- 6 spring onions, finely chopped
- 115 g/4 oz Cheddar cheese, grated
- salt and pepper (optional)
- crusty bread, to serve

Method

1. Brush the aubergine slices on one side with oil. Heat half the oil in a large heavy-based frying pan. Add the aubergine slices, oiled-side up, and cook over a medium heat for 5–6 minutes, or until browned on one side. Turn the slices over, cook on the other side until browned and transfer to a plate. Cut into bite-sized pieces and set aside.

2. Heat the remaining oil in a large saucepan over a medium heat. Add the onion and peppers and cook, stirring occasionally, for 3–4 minutes, or until the onion is just softened. Add the garlic and cook for a further 2–3 minutes, or until the onion just begins to colour.

3. Add the tomatoes, chilli powder, cumin and oregano. Season to taste with salt and pepper, if using. Bring just to the boil, reduce the heat, cover and simmer gently for 15 minutes.

4. Add the courgettes, aubergine and kidney beans. Stir in the water and tomato purée. Return to the boil, cover the saucepan and simmer for a further 45 minutes, or until the vegetables are tender. Taste and adjust the seasoning, adding salt and pepper, if needed.

5. Ladle into bowls and top with the spring onions and cheese. Serve with crusty bread.

VEGETABLES

CAULIFLOWER & SWEET POTATO CURRY

Serves: 4   **Prep: 20 mins**   **Cook: 40 mins**

Ingredients

- 4 tbsp ghee or vegetable oil
- 2 onions, finely chopped
- 1 tsp Panch Phoran
- 1 cauliflower, broken into small florets
- 350 g/12 oz sweet potatoes, diced
- 2 fresh green chillies, deseeded and finely chopped
- 1 tsp ginger paste
- 2 tsp paprika
- 1½ tsp ground cumin
- 1 tsp ground turmeric
- ½ tsp chilli powder
- 3 tomatoes, quartered
- 225 g/8 oz fresh or frozen peas
- 3 tbsp natural yogurt
- 225 ml/8 fl oz vegetable stock or water
- salt (optional)
- 1 tsp garam masala
- fresh coriander sprigs, to garnish

Method

1. Heat the ghee in a large, heavy-based frying pan. Add the onions and Panch Phoran and cook over a low heat, stirring frequently, for 10 minutes, or until the onions are golden. Add the cauliflower, sweet potatoes and chillies and cook, stirring frequently, for 3 minutes.

2. Stir in the ginger paste, paprika, cumin, turmeric and chilli powder and cook, stirring constantly, for 3 minutes. Add the tomatoes and peas and stir in the yogurt and stock. Season with salt to taste, if using, cover and simmer for 20 minutes, or until the vegetables are tender.

3. Sprinkle the garam masala over the curry, transfer to a warmed serving dish and serve immediately, garnished with fresh coriander sprigs.

VEGETABLES

SHAKSHOUKA

Serves: 4 **Prep: 20 mins** **Cook: 45 mins**

Ingredients

3 tbsp olive oil

1 tsp cumin seeds

2 red onions, thinly sliced

2 garlic cloves, finely chopped

1 red chilli, deseeded and finely chopped

1 tsp sea salt flakes, plus a pinch

2 red peppers, deseeded and thinly sliced

3 vine tomatoes, roughly chopped

2 pinches of pepper

4 eggs

2 tsp za'atar spice

Method

1. Preheat the oven to 180°C/350°F/Gas Mark 4. Heat the oil in a large ovenproof frying pan over a low heat. Add the cumin and fry for 1–2 minutes, or until aromatic. Add the red onions, garlic, chilli and 1 teaspoon of salt and fry for 5 minutes, or until softened, stirring often.

2. Add the red peppers and increase the heat to medium. Fry for 1 minute, stirring constantly. Reduce the heat to low, cover and cook for a further 20 minutes, stirring occasionally.

3. Add the tomatoes and a pinch of salt and pepper and cook for 5 minutes.

4. Using a wooden spoon, make four deep egg-sized indentations in the sauce, then crack an egg into each one. Sprinkle the za'atar over the eggs and sauce.

5. Bake for 10 minutes, or until just set. Sprinkle over the remaining pinch of pepper and serve hot.

VEGETABLES

BRAISED PEAS WITH LETTUCE & TARRAGON

Serves: 4 **Prep: 5 mins** **Cook: 10–15 mins**

Ingredients

15 g/½ oz butter
1 tbsp olive oil
1 leek, thinly sliced
2 tsp plain flour
250 ml/9 fl oz vegetable stock
375 g/13 oz fresh or frozen peas
2 large Little Gem lettuces, sliced
3 tbsp chopped fresh tarragon
1 tbsp lemon juice
salt and pepper (optional)

Method

1. Heat the butter and oil in a large saucepan. Add the leek, cover and cook over a low heat for 5 minutes, until soft. Stir in the flour, then gradually stir in the stock.

2. Add the peas, increase the heat, cover and simmer for 4 minutes. Add the lettuce without stirring it in, cover and simmer for a further 2 minutes, until the vegetables are tender.

3. Stir the lettuce, tarragon and lemon juice into the peas. Season with salt and pepper, if using, and serve immediately.

VEGETABLES

AUBERGINE GRATIN

Serves: 2 **Prep: 25 mins** **Cook: 40–50 mins**

Ingredients

- 4 tbsp olive oil
- 2 onions, finely chopped
- 2 garlic cloves, very finely chopped
- 2 aubergines, thickly sliced
- 3 tbsp chopped fresh flat-leaf parsley, plus extra sprigs to garnish
- ½ tsp dried thyme
- 400 g/14 oz canned chopped tomatoes
- 175 g/6 oz mozzarella cheese, coarsely grated
- 6 tbsp freshly grated Parmesan cheese
- salt and pepper (optional)

Method

1. Heat the oil in a flameproof casserole over a medium heat. Add the onions and cook for 5 minutes, or until soft.

2. Add the garlic and cook for a few seconds, or until just beginning to colour. Using a slotted spoon, transfer the onion mixture to a plate. Add the aubergine slices to the casserole in batches and cook until lightly browned. Transfer to a separate plate.

3. Preheat the oven to 200°C/400°F/Gas Mark 6. Arrange a layer of aubergine slices in the base of the casserole. Sprinkle with some of the parsley, thyme, and salt and pepper to taste, if using.

4. Add layers of onion, tomatoes and mozzarella cheese, sprinkling parsley, thyme, and salt and pepper to taste over each layer. Continue layering, finishing with a layer of aubergine slices. Sprinkle with the Parmesan cheese and bake, uncovered, in the preheated oven for 20–30 minutes, or until the top is golden and the aubergines are tender. Serve hot, garnished with parsley sprigs.

VEGETABLES

VEGETABLE PHO

Serves: 4 **Prep: 10 mins** **Cook: 30 mins**

Ingredients

1.5 litres/2½ pints gluten-free reduced-salt vegetable stock

2 tbsp tamari

2 garlic cloves, thinly sliced

2.5-cm/1-inch piece ginger, peeled and thinly sliced

1 cinnamon stick

1 bay leaf

1 carrot, cut into thin batons

1 small fennel bulb, thinly sliced

150 g/5½ oz vermicelli rice noodles

85 g/3 oz button mushrooms, sliced

115 g/4 oz beansprouts

4 spring onions, thinly sliced diagonally

3 tbsp chopped fresh coriander

fresh basil leaves, chopped red chillies, lime wedges and tamari, to serve

Method

1. Place the stock in a large pan with the tamari, garlic, ginger, cinnamon and bay leaf. Bring to the boil, reduce the heat, cover and simmer for about 20 minutes.

2. Add the carrot and fennel and simmer for 1 minute. Add the noodles and simmer for a further 4 minutes.

3. Add the mushrooms, beansprouts and spring onions and return to the boil

4. Ladle into warmed soup bowls and sprinkle with the coriander. Remove and discard the bay leaf and cinnamon. Serve immediately with basil leaves, chillies, lime wedges and tamari.

VEGETABLES

PERSIAN HERB FRITTATA

Serves: 2 **Prep: 15 mins** **Cook: 10 mins**

Ingredients

6 eggs
2 tbsp finely chopped fresh dill
6 tbsp finely chopped fresh flat-leaf parsley
6 tbsp finely chopped fresh coriander
2 tbsp finely chopped fresh mint
2 garlic cloves, crushed
1 tbsp plain flour
¼ tsp ground turmeric
large pinch of sea salt
large pinch of pepper
20 g/¾ oz butter
1 tbsp olive oil
30 g/1 oz walnuts, chopped
1 spring onion, thinly sliced, to garnish

Method

1. Preheat the oven to 180°C/350°F/Gas Mark 4. Crack the eggs into a large bowl. Add the herbs, garlic, flour, turmeric, salt and pepper, then whisk well.

2. Heat the butter with the oil in a large, heavy-based, ovenproof frying pan over a medium–high heat until foaming. As soon as it stops foaming, pour in the egg mixture, reduce the heat to medium–low and cook for 5 minutes.

3. Scatter the walnuts over the frittata, then transfer the frying pan to the oven and bake for 5 minutes, or until cooked through.

4. Using oven gloves, turn the frittata out onto a plate. Scatter with the spring onion, then cut into wedges and serve.

VEGETABLES

HOT & SOUR NOODLES WITH TOFU

Serves: 4 **Prep: 15 mins** **Cook: 20 mins**

Ingredients

3 strips lime rind

2 garlic cloves, peeled

2 slices fresh ginger

1 litre/1¾ pints chicken stock

1 tbsp vegetable oil

150 g/5½ oz firm tofu (drained weight), cubed

200 g/7 oz dried fine egg noodles

100 g/3½ oz shiitake mushrooms, sliced

1 fresh red chilli, deseeded and sliced

4 spring onions, sliced

1 tsp soy sauce

juice of 1 lime

1 tsp Chinese rice wine

1 tsp sesame oil

chopped fresh coriander, to garnish

Method

1. Put the lime rind, garlic and ginger into a large saucepan with the stock and bring to the boil. Reduce the heat and simmer for 5 minutes. Remove the lime rind, garlic and ginger with a slotted spoon and discard.

2. Meanwhile, heat the vegetable oil in a large frying pan over a high heat, add the tofu and cook, turning frequently, until golden. Remove from the pan and drain on kitchen paper.

3. Add the noodles, mushrooms and chilli to the stock and simmer for 3 minutes. Add the tofu, spring onions, soy sauce, lime juice, rice wine and sesame oil and briefly heat through.

4. Divide between 4 warmed bowls, scatter over the coriander and serve immediately.

VEGETABLES

SQUASH, KALE & FARRO STEW

Serves: 6 **Prep: 30 mins** **Cook: 55 mins**

Ingredients

1 dense-fleshed squash, such as Kabocha or Crown Prince, weighing about 1.25 kg/2 lb 12 oz

2 tbsp vegetable oil

1 onion, finely chopped

2 tsp dried oregano

2 garlic cloves, finely sliced

400 g/14 oz canned chopped tomatoes

700 ml/1¼ pints vegetable stock

125 g/4½ oz quick-cook farro, rinsed

250 g/9 oz kale, sliced into ribbons

400 g/14 oz canned chickpeas, drained and rinsed

6 tbsp chopped fresh coriander

juice of 1 lime

salt and pepper (optional)

Method

1. Cut the squash into quarters, peel and deseed. Cut the flesh into large cubes (you will need about 650 g/1 lb 7 oz).

2. Heat the oil in a flameproof casserole or heavy-based saucepan. Add the onion and fry over a medium heat for 5 minutes, until translucent. Add the oregano and garlic and fry for 2 minutes.

3. Add the squash and cook, covered, for 10 minutes.

4. Add the tomatoes, stock and farro, cover and bring to the boil. Reduce the heat to a gentle simmer and cook for 20 minutes, stirring occasionally.

5. Add the kale and chickpeas. Cook for a further 15 minutes, or until the kale is just tender.

6. Season to taste with salt and pepper, if using. Stir in the coriander and lime juice just before serving.

★ Variation

You can replace some of the squash content with potatoes, peeled and cut into large cubes.

VEGETABLES

BEANS

MEXICAN BLACK BEAN PAN-FRY	208
SWEET POTATO & CHICKPEA CURRY	210
LENTIL QUINOA POT	212
MEXICAN BEEF & BEAN BOWL	214
RED KIDNEY BEAN CURRY	216
PUMPKIN & HARICOT BEAN SOUP	218
PRAWN & FERMENTED BLACK BEAN SOUP	219
CAULIFLOWER & BUTTERBEAN STEW	220
SPICY CHICKPEA & RED PEPPER SOUP	222
TUSCAN BEAN STEW	224
SPLIT PEA & HAM SOUP	226
CAULIFLOWER DHAL SOUP	228
CHILLI BEAN STEW	229
JERK TURKEY & BLACK-EYED BEAN SOUP	230
SPICY BEAN CHILLI	231
HARICOT BEANS & VEGETABLE CASSEROLE	232
CHICKEN, SQUASH & BEAN CASSEROLE	234
LENTIL & RICE CASSEROLE	236
RIBOLLITA	238
KIDNEY BEAN, PUMPKIN & TOMATO STEW	240
MOROCCAN VEGETABLE & CHICKPEA STEW	242
HAM & BLACK-EYED BEAN STEW	244
VEGETABLE & LENTIL CASSEROLE	246
BEAN & TOMATO CASSEROLE WITH PARMESAN TOASTS	247
VEGETABLE & PUY GOULASH	248
LENTIL BOLOGNAISE	250
SPICY AUBERGINE & CHICKPEA CASSEROLE	252

MEXICAN BLACK BEAN PAN-FRY

Serves: 4 **Prep: 12 mins** **Cook: 30–35 mins**

Ingredients

- 1 tbsp olive oil
- 1 onion, diced
- 2 garlic cloves, crushed
- 500 g/1 lb 2 oz fresh turkey mince
- 2 tsp ground cumin
- 1 tsp smoked paprika
- 400 g/14 oz canned chopped tomatoes
- 200 ml/7 fl oz chicken stock
- 1 tbsp tomato purée
- 400 g/14 oz canned black beans, drained
- 100 g/3½ oz tortillas chips
- 2 spring onions, trimmed and chopped
- 100 g/3½ oz frozen sweetcorn, thawed
- 75 g/2¾ oz Cheddar cheese, grated
- salt and pepper (optional)

Method

1. Heat the oil in a large frying pan, add the onion and sauté for 3–4 minutes, then stir in the garlic and cook for a further minute.
2. Add the mince and cook, breaking it up with a wooden spoon, for 5–6 minutes, until brown all over.
3. Stir in the cumin and paprika, then add the chopped tomatoes, stock and tomato purée and stir in the beans. Season to taste with salt and pepper, if using. Bring to the boil, reduce the heat and simmer for 15–20 minutes, until the chilli has a sauce-like consistency.
4. Preheat the grill to medium. Layer the tortilla chips on top of the chilli and sprinkle with the spring onions, sweetcorn and cheese. Cook under the grill until the cheese is bubbling and golden.

★ Variation

The turkey mince gives you a lean chilli – you can use fresh beef mince for a more traditional chilli.

BEANS

SWEET POTATO & CHICKPEA CURRY

Serves: 4 **Prep: 8 mins** **Cook: 17–20 mins**

Ingredients

- 1 tbsp coconut oil
- 1 tsp mustard seeds
- 1 tsp cumin seeds
- 2 garlic cloves, crushed
- 2 tsp Thai green curry paste
- 400 ml/14 fl oz canned coconut milk
- 100 ml/3½ fl oz water
- 500 g/1 lb 2 oz sweet potatoes, peeled and chopped
- 400 g/14 oz canned chickpeas, drained
- 100 g/3½ oz spinach leaves
- 2 tbsp cashew nuts, toasted
- handful of fresh coriander leaves, roughly chopped
- 4 flatbreads, to serve

Method

1. Heat the oil in a large wok or frying pan, add the mustard and cumin seeds and heat until they start to pop.
2. Stir in the garlic and curry paste and cook, stirring for 1 minute.
3. Pour in the coconut milk and water and bring to the boil.
4. Add the sweet potatoes and chickpeas and simmer for 12–15 minutes, until the sweet potatoes are tender.
5. Stir in the spinach, cashew nuts and half the coriander and cook for 2 minutes, until the spinach is wilted.
6. Sprinkle with the remaining coriander and serve with the flatbreads.

★ Variation

Any canned beans, such as butter beans, pinto beans or kidney beans, can be used instead of chickpeas if you don't have them.

BEANS

LENTIL QUINOA POT

Serves: 4 **Prep: 8 mins** **Cook: 20–22 mins**

Ingredients

- 1 tbsp coconut oil
- 100 g/3½ oz quinoa
- 4 spring onions, trimmed and sliced
- 175 g/6 oz tenderstem broccoli, trimmed and halved
- 500 ml/18 fl oz vegetable stock
- 100 g/3½ oz frozen soya beans, thawed
- 400 g/14 oz canned green lentils, drained
- 1 tsp harissa
- 2 tbsp flaked almonds, toasted
- seeds from ½ pomegranate
- 100 g/3½ oz feta cheese, crumbled
- 2 tbsp chopped fresh coriander
- salt and pepper (optional)

Method

1. Heat the coconut oil in a wok or large frying pan, add the quinoa and toast until golden.
2. Add the spring onions and broccoli, then pour in the stock. Bring to the boil and simmer for 10–12 minutes.
3. When almost all of the stock has been absorbed stir in the beans, lentils and harissa and cook until all the liquid has been absorbed. Season to taste with salt and pepper, if using.
4. Sprinkle with the flaked almonds, pomegranate seeds, cheese and coriander and serve immediately.

BEANS

MEXICAN BEEF & BEAN BOWL

Serves: 4 **Prep: 10 mins** **Cook: 20-25 mins**

Ingredients

1 tbsp olive oil

500 g/1 lb 2 oz fresh beef mince

1 onion, chopped

2 red peppers, deseeded and sliced

2½ tsp chilli powder

400 g/14 oz canned red kidney beans, drained

400 g/14 oz canned cannellini beans, drained

400 g/14 oz canned chopped tomatoes

1 tbsp tomato purée

100 ml/3½ fl oz vegetable stock

200 g/7 oz basmati rice

2 tbsp chopped fresh coriander

2 tbsp soured cream and ¼ tsp smoked paprika, to serve

salt and pepper (optional)

Method

1. Heat the oil in a large frying pan, add the mince and cook for 2–3 minutes, until brown all over.

2. Add the onion and red peppers and cook, stirring occasionally, for 3–4 minutes.

3. Stir in the chilli powder and cook for 1 minute, then add the kidney beans, cannellini beans, tomatoes, tomato purée and stock. Bring to a simmer and simmer for 12–15 minutes. Season to taste with salt and pepper, if using.

4. Meanwhile, cook the rice according to the packet instructions.

5. Stir the coriander into the chilli and serve in warmed bowls with the rice, topped with a dollop of soured cream and a sprinkling of smoked paprika.

BEANS

RED KIDNEY BEAN CURRY

Serves: 4 **Prep: 20 mins** **Cook: 30–35 mins**

Ingredients

- 2 tbsp vegetable or groundnut oil
- 2 tsp cumin seeds
- 2 onions, finely chopped
- 2 tsp grated fresh ginger
- 6 garlic cloves, crushed
- 2 fresh green chillies, finely chopped
- 2 large tomatoes, roughly chopped
- 2 tsp ground coriander
- 1 tsp ground cumin
- ¼ tsp ground turmeric
- 1 tsp garam masala
- 800 g/1 lb 12 oz canned red kidney beans, drained and rinsed
- 1 tsp palm sugar
- 500 ml/18 fl oz warm water
- 1 tsp salt
- 4 tbsp finely chopped fresh coriander, to garnish
- 2 tbsp natural yogurt, to serve

Method

1. Heat the oil in a large saucepan and add the cumin seeds. When they stop crackling, add the onions and fry until soft.

2. Add the ginger and garlic and fry for 2 minutes. Add the chillies, tomatoes, ground coriander, cumin, turmeric and garam masala and stir-fry for 12–15 minutes.

3. Add the red kidney beans, palm sugar, water and salt and cook for 10–12 minutes, or until the beans are soft.

4. Remove from the heat and transfer to a serving dish. Garnish with the chopped coriander and serve with the yogurt.

BEANS

PUMPKIN & HARICOT BEAN SOUP

Serves: 4 **Prep: 20–25 mins** **Cook: 30–40 mins**

Ingredients

- 1 tsp olive oil
- 1 red onion, chopped
- 2 garlic cloves, crushed
- 450 g/1 lb pumpkin, peeled, deseeded and chopped into small cubes
- 2 tsp smoked paprika
- ¼ tsp dried chilli flakes
- 5–6 fresh sage leaves, finely chopped
- 850 ml/1½ pints vegetable stock
- 400 g/14 oz canned haricot beans, drained and rinsed
- salt and pepper (optional)
- 2 tbsp finely chopped, fresh flat-leaf parsley, to garnish

Method

1. Heat the oil in a saucepan and fry the onion and garlic for 3–4 minutes. Add the pumpkin and cook for a further 4–5 minutes.

2. Add the paprika, chilli and sage and cook for 1 minute, stirring all the time.

3. Pour in the stock and season to taste with salt and pepper, if using. Cover and simmer for 20–25 minutes, or until the pumpkin is tender. Allow the soup to cool slightly then process, using a hand-held blender, until smooth.

4. Stir in the haricot beans and heat through for 2–3 minutes. Ladle into warmed bowls, garnish with the parsley and serve immediately.

BEANS

PRAWN & FERMENTED BLACK BEAN SOUP

Serves: 4 **Prep: 15 mins** **Cook: 15 mins**

Ingredients

- 1 litre/1¾ pints vegetable stock
- 1 tbsp fermented black bean paste
- 25 g/1 oz fresh ginger, peeled and finely chopped
- 1 kaffir lime leaf, 4 spring onions, thinly sliced and 2 tsp tamari
- 2 tsp clear honey
- 250 g/9 oz frozen cooked peeled tiger prawns, thawed, rinsed and drained
- 115 g/4 oz frozen edamame beans
- 115 g/4 oz baby corn, sliced
- 70 g/2½ oz young Swiss chard leaves
- 20 g/¾ oz fresh coriander
- 2 tsp sesame seeds, toasted

Method

1. Add the stock, bean paste, ginger, lime leaf and spring onions to a medium-sized saucepan. Stir in the tamari and honey and bring to the boil, then cover and simmer for 5 minutes.

2. Add the prawns and beans and cook for 3 minutes, then add the baby corn and chard. Cook for 2 minutes until the chard has just wilted and the prawns are piping hot.

3. Chop the coriander, stir it in to the pan and sprinkle with the sesame seeds. Ladle into warmed bowls and serve immediately.

BEANS

CAULIFLOWER & BUTTER BEAN STEW

Serves: 4 **Prep: 10 mins** **Cook: 35 mins**

Ingredients

- 2 tbsp olive oil
- 2 large red onions, sliced
- 2 carrots, cut into 2-cm/ ¾-inch dice
- 2 celery sticks, cut into 2-cm/¾-inch dice
- 3 garlic cloves, crushed
- 400 g/14 oz canned plum tomatoes in juice
- 250 ml/9 fl oz vegetable stock
- 1 tbsp sun-dried tomato purée
- ½ tbsp dried mixed herbs
- ½ tsp pepper
- salt (optional)
- 800 g/1 lb 12 oz canned butter beans, drained and rinsed
- 1 head cauliflower, divided into florets
- 1 tsp sweet paprika, to garnish

Method

1. Add the oil to a large lidded saucepan and place over a medium–hot heat. Add the onions, carrots and celery and cook for 5 minutes, or until lightly coloured, stirring from time to time. Stir in the garlic and cook for a minute.

2. Add the canned tomatoes, roughly crushing any whole ones against the sides of the pan, and their juice. Stir in the stock, tomato purée, herbs, pepper and salt, if using. Bring to a simmer, reduce the heat to low and place the lid on. Cook for 20 minutes, or until all the vegetables are tender.

3. Stir in the butter beans and cook for a further 5 minutes. Place the cauliflower florets on top of the stew, put the lid back on and simmer for 5 minutes more, or until the cauliflower is just tender when the stalks are pierced with a sharp knife.

4. Serve the stew immediately, garnished with the sweet paprika.

BEANS

SPICY CHICKPEA & RED PEPPER SOUP

Serves: 4 **Prep: 15 mins** **Cook: 25 mins**

Ingredients

- 2½ tbsp olive oil
- 6 spring onions, chopped
- 1 large fresh red jalapeño chilli, deseeded and finely sliced
- 4 garlic cloves, finely chopped
- 2 tsp ground cumin
- 1 tsp chilli powder
- 3 fresh ripe tomatoes, peeled and roughly chopped
- 400 g/14 oz ready-roasted red peppers in water, drained and thinly sliced
- 1 tbsp red pepper pesto
- 1 litre/1¾ pints reduced-salt vegetable stock
- 400 g/14 oz canned chickpeas, drained and rinsed
- 1 tsp stevia granules
- 2 tsp red wine vinegar
- 100 g/3½ oz baby spinach leaves
- pepper (optional)
- oat bread, to serve

Method

1. Heat the oil in a large saucepan over a medium heat. Add the spring onions and cook for 2–3 minutes, stirring occasionally, until soft.
2. Add the chilli, garlic, cumin and chilli powder and cook for 1 minute, stirring.
3. Stir in the tomatoes, red peppers, pesto and stock and bring to a simmer. Cook for 10 minutes, then add the chickpeas, stevia granules, vinegar and pepper, if using, and cook for a further 5 minutes.
4. Stir in the spinach and cook for 1 minute, until the spinach wilts. Serve with the oat bread.

★ Variation

You can replace the spinach leaves with the same quantity of kale. You can also create a thicker soup by tipping half of the soup into a blender at the end of step 3 (before adding the spinach) and blend. Return to the pan with the rest of the soup and stir well.

BEANS

TUSCAN BEAN STEW

Serves: 4 **Prep: 25 mins** **Cook: 45–50 mins**

Ingredients

1 large fennel bulb

2 tbsp olive oil

1 red onion, cut into small wedges

2–4 garlic cloves, sliced

1 fresh green chilli, deseeded and chopped

1 small aubergine, about 225 g/8 oz, cut into chunks

2 tbsp tomato purée

450–600 ml/16 fl oz–1 pint vegetable stock

450 g/1 lb ripe tomatoes

1 tbsp balsamic vinegar

a few fresh oregano sprigs

400 g/14 oz canned borlotti beans

400 g/14 oz canned flageolet beans

1 yellow pepper, deseeded and cut into small strips

1 courgette, sliced into half moons

55 g/2 oz stoned black olives

25 g/1 oz Parmesan cheese shavings

salt and pepper (optional)

crusty bread, to serve

Method

1. Trim the fennel and reserve any feathery fronds, then cut the bulb into small strips. Heat the oil in a large heavy-based saucepan with a tight-fitting lid and cook the onion, garlic, chilli and fennel strips, stirring frequently, for 5–8 minutes, or until softened.

2. Add the aubergine and cook, stirring frequently, for 5 minutes. Blend the tomato purée with a little of the stock in a jug and pour into the pan, then add the remaining stock, the tomatoes, vinegar and oregano. Bring to the boil, then reduce the heat, cover and simmer for 15 minutes, or until the tomatoes have begun to collapse.

3. Drain and rinse the beans, then drain again. Add them to the pan with the yellow pepper, courgette and olives. Simmer for a further 15 minutes, or until all the vegetables are tender. Taste and adjust the seasoning, adding salt and pepper if needed. Scatter with the Parmesan shavings and serve immediately, garnished with the reserved fennel fronds and accompanied by crusty bread.

BEANS

SPLIT PEA & HAM SOUP

Serves: 6 **Prep: 15–20 mins** **Cook: 1 hour 20 mins –1 hour 50 mins**

Ingredients

- 500 g/1 lb 2 oz split green peas
- 1 tbsp olive oil
- 1 large onion, finely chopped
- 1 large carrot, finely chopped
- 1 celery stick, finely chopped
- 1 litre/1¾ pints chicken stock or vegetable stock
- 1 litre/1¾ pints water
- 225 g/8 oz lean smoked ham, finely diced
- ¼ tsp dried thyme
- ¼ tsp dried marjoram
- 1 bay leaf
- salt and pepper (optional)

Method

1. Rinse the peas under cold running water. Put them in a saucepan and cover generously with water. Bring to the boil and boil for 3 minutes, skimming off the foam from the surface. Drain the peas.

2. Heat the oil in a large saucepan over a medium heat. Add the onion and cook for 3–4 minutes, stirring occasionally, until just softened. Add the carrot and celery and continue cooking for 2 minutes.

3. Add the peas, pour over the stock and water and stir to combine.

4. Bring just to the boil and stir the ham into the soup. Add the thyme, marjoram and bay leaf. Reduce the heat, cover and cook gently for 1–1½ hours, until the ingredients are very soft. Remove and discard the bay leaf.

5. Taste and add salt and pepper, if using. Ladle into warmed bowls and serve immediately.

BEANS

CAULIFLOWER DHAL SOUP

Serves: 4 **Prep:** 20 mins **Cook:** 45–50 mins

Ingredients

- 1 tbsp sunflower oil
- 1 onion, finely chopped
- 1 cauliflower, cut into small florets
- 1 tsp coriander seeds, roughly crushed
- 1 tsp cumin seeds, roughly crushed
- 1 tsp black mustard seeds
- 1 tsp turmeric
- 1 litre/1¾ pints vegetable stock
- 150 g/5½ oz red lentils
- ¼ tsp salt
- large pinch of pepper (optional)
- 4 tbsp chopped fresh coriander

Method

1. Heat the oil in a saucepan, add the onion and fry over a medium heat, stirring occasionally, for 5 minutes until soft. Add the cauliflower, coriander seeds, cumin seeds, black mustard seeds and turmeric, stir well to coat the cauliflower in the spices, then fry for 2–3 minutes until the cauliflower is coloured and just beginning to brown around the edges. Scoop out some of the cauliflower florets and reserve to garnish.

2. Pour the stock into the saucepan, add the lentils, salt and pepper, if using, and bring to the boil, stirring. Reduce the heat, cover and simmer for 30–35 minutes, stirring occasionally until the lentils are soft.

3. Roughly mash the soup, then stir in the chopped coriander. Ladle into warmed bowls, top with the reserved cauliflower florets and serve immediately.

BEANS

CHILLI BEAN STEW

Serves: 4 **Prep: 25 mins** **Cook: 36–46 mins**

Ingredients

- 1 onion and 2–4 garlic cloves
- 2 fresh red chillies
- 2 tbsp olive oil
- 225 g/8 oz canned kidney beans, 225 g/8 oz canned cannellini beans and 225 g/8 oz canned chickpeas
- 1 tbsp tomato purée
- 900 ml/1½ pints vegetable stock
- 1 red pepper
- 4 tomatoes
- 175 g/6 oz shelled fresh broad beans
- 1 tbsp fresh coriander, plus extra to garnish
- paprika, to garnish, and soured cream, to serve (optional)

Method

1. Chop the onion and garlic cloves and deseed and slice the chillies.
2. Heat the oil in a large, heavy-based saucepan with a tight-fitting lid. Add the onion, garlic and chillies and cook, stirring frequently, for 5 minutes until soft.
3. Drain and rinse the kidney beans, cannellini beans and chickpeas and add to the pan. Blend the tomato purée with a little of the stock and pour over the bean mixture, then add the remaining stock.
4. Bring to the boil, then reduce the heat and simmer for 10–15 minutes. Deseed and chop the red pepper. and chop the tomatoes. Then add the red pepper, tomatoes and broad beans.
5. Simmer for a further 15–20 minutes or until all the vegetables are tender. Stir in most of the chopped coriander.
6. Serve the stew immediately, garnished with the remaining coriander, a pinch of paprika and a spoonful of soured cream, if using.

BEANS

JERK TURKEY & BLACK-EYED BEAN SOUP

Serves: 4 **Prep: 25–30 mins** **Cook: 40 mins**

Ingredients

- 1 tbsp olive oil, 1 onion and 2 garlic cloves, finely chopped
- 2-cm/¾-inch piece ginger, peeled and chopped
- ¼ tsp grated nutmeg, ½ tsp ground allspice and ½ tsp dried crushed red chillies
- 2 tsp ground cumin and 2 tsp fresh thyme leaves
- 450 g/1 lb tomatoes, peeled and chopped
- 600 ml/1 pint turkey stock
- 1 tbsp tomato purée
- 1 tbsp muscovado sugar
- 400 g/14 oz canned black-eyed beans, drained
- 280 g/10 oz turkey breast
- 2 tbsp fresh coriander
- salt and pepper (optional)

Method

1. Heat the oil in a saucepan over a medium heat, add the onion and fry, stirring, for 5 minutes until just beginning to colour. Sprinkle over the garlic and ginger, then add the nutmeg, allspice, chillies and cumin. Add the thyme and tomatoes and mix together well.

2. Pour in the stock, add the tomato purée, sugar, beans and turkey pieces and bring to the boil. Cover and simmer for 30 minutes or until the turkey pieces are cooked through with no hint of pink juices when pierced in the thickest parts with a knife. Lift the turkey pieces out of the pan, transfer to a plate and tear into shreds with two forks.

3. Chop the coriander and stir it into the soup with salt and pepper to taste, if using. Ladle into warmed bowls, then top with the shreds of turkey and serve immediately.

BEANS

SPICY BEAN CHILLI

Serves: 4   **Prep: 20 mins**   **Cook: 20 mins**

Ingredients

- 1 large onion
- 1 large green pepper
- 2 garlic cloves
- 2 tbsp olive oil
- 2 tsp dried crushed chillies
- 400 g/14 oz canned chopped plum tomatoes
- 300 g/10½ oz canned red kidney beans, drained
- 300 g/10½ oz canned cannellini beans, drained
- 3 tbsp chopped fresh coriander
- salt and pepper (optional)
- tortilla chips, to serve

Method

1. Chop the onion, deseed and chop the green pepper and crush the garlic. Heat the oil in a large frying pan over a medium heat. Add the onion and green pepper and stir-fry for 8 minutes until soft and light brown.

2. Stir in the garlic and chillies, then add the tomatoes and simmer for 2 minutes.

3. Add the kidney beans, cannellini beans and coriander, bring to the boil, then reduce the heat and simmer for 5 minutes. Season to taste with salt and pepper, if using.

4. Transfer to warmed serving bowls and serve immediately with tortilla chips.

BEANS

HARICOT BEANS & VEGETABLE CASSEROLE

Serves: 8

Prep: 20–25 mins plus overnight soaking

Cook: 2¼ hours–2 hours 20 mins

Ingredients

650 g/1 lb 7 oz dried haricot beans, soaked overnight and drained (it is important to pre-soak the beans before cooking them in step 1)

2 bay leaves

3 onions

4 cloves

1 tbsp olive oil

4 garlic cloves, finely chopped

4 leeks, sliced

800 g/1 lb 12 oz baby carrots

225 g/8 oz button mushrooms

800 g/1 lb 12 oz canned chopped tomatoes

4 tbsp chopped fresh parsley

1 tbsp chopped fresh savory

115 g/4 oz fresh breadcrumbs

salt and pepper (optional)

Method

1. Put the beans and bay leaves into a saucepan. Stud one of the onions with the cloves and add to the pan. Pour in enough water to cover and bring to the boil. Reduce the heat, cover and simmer for 1 hour, then drain, reserving the cooking liquid. Remove and discard the bay leaves and onion.

2. Preheat the oven to 180°C/350°F/Gas Mark 4.

3. Chop the remaining onions. Heat the oil in a flameproof casserole, then add the chopped onions, garlic and leeks and cook over a low heat, stirring occasionally, for 5 minutes, until softened.

4. Add the carrots, mushrooms and tomatoes, pour in 850 ml/1½ pints of the reserved cooking liquid and season to taste with salt and pepper, if using. Bring to the boil, then reduce the heat, cover and simmer for 15 minutes.

5. Stir in the beans, parsley and savory and adjust the seasoning, adding salt and pepper if needed. Sprinkle with the breadcrumbs and transfer the casserole to the preheated oven. Bake, uncovered, for 40–45 minutes, until the topping is golden brown. Serve immediately.

BEANS

CHICKEN, SQUASH & BEAN CASSEROLE

Serves: 4 **Prep: 20 mins** **Cook: 1 hour 20 mins–1 hour 35 mins**

Ingredients

2 tbsp olive oil

4 skinless, boneless chicken thighs, about 100 g/3½ oz each, cut into bite-sized pieces

1 large onion, sliced

2 leeks, chopped

2 garlic cloves, chopped

1 butternut squash, peeled, deseeded and cut into cubes

2 carrots, diced

400 g/14 oz canned chopped tomatoes with herbs

400 g/14 oz canned mixed beans, drained and rinsed

100 ml/3½ fl oz vegetable or chicken stock, plus extra if needed

salt and pepper (optional)

Method

1. Preheat the oven to 160°C/325°F/Gas Mark 3.
2. Heat half the oil in a large flameproof casserole over a high heat, add the chicken and cook, turning frequently, for 2–3 minutes, until browned all over. Reduce the heat to medium, remove the chicken with a slotted spoon and set aside.
3. Add the remaining oil to the casserole, add the onion and leeks and cook, stirring occasionally, for 10 minutes, or until soft. Add the garlic, squash and carrots and cook, stirring, for 2 minutes. Add the tomatoes, beans and stock, stir well and bring to a simmer. Return the chicken to the casserole.
4. Cover, transfer to the preheated oven and cook for 1–1¼ hours, stirring once or twice. If the casserole looks too dry, add a little extra stock. Season to taste with salt and pepper, if using, and serve immediately.

BEANS

LENTIL & RICE CASSEROLE

Serves: 4 **Prep: 20 mins** **Cook: 35–40 mins**

Ingredients

- 225 g/8 oz red lentils
- 55 g/2 oz long-grain rice
- 1.2 litres/2 pints vegetable stock
- 1 leek, cut into chunks
- 3 garlic cloves, crushed
- 400 g/14 oz canned chopped tomatoes
- 1 tsp ground cumin
- 1 tsp chilli powder
- 1 tsp garam masala
- 1 red pepper, deseeded and sliced
- 100 g/3½ oz small broccoli florets
- 8 baby sweetcorn, halved lengthways
- 55 g/2 oz French beans, halved
- 1 tbsp shredded fresh basil
- salt and pepper (optional)
- fresh basil sprigs, to garnish

Method

1. Place the lentils, rice and stock in a large flameproof casserole and cook over a low heat, stirring occasionally, for 20 minutes.
2. Add the leek, garlic, tomatoes and their can juice, ground cumin, chilli powder, garam masala, sliced pepper, broccoli, baby sweetcorn and French beans to the pan.
3. Bring the mixture to the boil, reduce the heat, cover and simmer for a further 10–15 minutes or until the vegetables are tender.
4. Add the shredded basil and season to taste with salt and pepper, if using. Garnish with fresh basil sprigs and serve immediately.

BEANS

RIBOLLITA

Serves: 4 **Prep: 20 mins** **Cook: 45–50 mins**

Ingredients

3 tbsp olive oil

2 medium red onions, roughly chopped

3 carrots, sliced

3 celery sticks, roughly chopped

3 garlic cloves, chopped

1 tbsp chopped fresh thyme

400 g/14 oz canned cannellini beans, drained and rinsed

400 g/14 oz canned chopped tomatoes

600 ml/1 pint water or vegetable stock

2 tbsp chopped fresh parsley

500 g/1 lb 2 oz cavolo nero or Savoy cabbage, trimmed and sliced

1 small day-old ciabatta loaf, torn into small pieces

salt and pepper (optional)

extra virgin olive oil, to serve

Method

1. Heat the oil in a large saucepan and cook the onions, carrots and celery for 10–15 minutes, stirring frequently. Add the garlic, thyme, and salt and pepper to taste, if using. Continue to cook for a further 1–2 minutes, until the vegetables are golden and caramelized.

2. Add the cannellini beans to the pan and pour in the tomatoes.

3. Add enough of the water to cover the vegetables. Bring to the boil and simmer for 20 minutes. Add the parsley and cavolo nero and cook for a further 5 minutes.

4. Stir in the bread and add a little more water, if needed. The consistency should be thick.

5. Taste and add salt and pepper, if needed. Ladle into warmed serving bowls and serve hot, drizzled with extra virgin olive oil.

KIDNEY BEAN, PUMPKIN & TOMATO STEW

Serves: 4–6

Prep: 20–25 mins
plus overnight soaking

Cook: 2 hours 25 mins

Ingredients

- 250 g/9 oz dried kidney beans (it is important to pre-soak the beans before cooking them – this is described in step 1)
- 1 tbsp olive oil
- 2 onions, finely chopped
- 4 garlic cloves, finely chopped
- 1 celery stick, thinly sliced
- 1 carrot, halved and thinly sliced
- 1.2 litres/2 pints water
- 2 tsp tomato purée
- 1/8 tsp dried thyme
- 1/8 tsp dried oregano
- 1/8 tsp ground cumin
- 1 bay leaf
- 400 g/14 oz canned chopped tomatoes
- 250 g/9 oz peeled pumpkin flesh, diced
- 1/4 tsp chilli purée, or to taste
- salt and pepper (optional)
- fresh coriander leaves, to garnish

Method

1. Pick over the beans, cover generously with cold water and leave to soak for 6 hours or overnight. Drain the beans, put in a saucepan and add enough cold water to cover by 5 cm/2 inches. Bring to the boil and boil for 10 minutes. Drain and rinse well.

2. Heat the oil in a large saucepan over a medium heat. Add the onions, cover and cook for 3–4 minutes, until they are just softened, stirring occasionally. Add the garlic, celery and carrot, and continue cooking for 2 minutes.

3. Add the water, drained beans, tomato purée, thyme, oregano, cumin and bay leaf. When the mixture begins to bubble, reduce the heat to low. Cover and simmer gently for 1 hour, stirring occasionally.

4. Stir in the tomatoes, pumpkin and chilli purée and continue simmering for a further hour, or until the beans and pumpkin are tender, stirring from time to time.

5. Season to taste with salt and pepper, if using, and stir in a little more chilli purée, if liked. Ladle the stew into warmed bowls, garnish with coriander and serve.

BEANS

MOROCCAN VEGETABLE & CHICKPEA STEW

Serves: 4 **Prep: 20 mins** **Cook: 45 mins**

Ingredients

2 tbsp olive oil

1 Spanish onion, finely chopped

2–4 garlic cloves, crushed

1 fresh red chilli, deseeded and sliced

1 aubergine, about 225 g/ 8 oz, cut into small chunks

small piece fresh ginger, peeled and grated

1 tsp ground cumin

1 tsp ground coriander

pinch of saffron threads or ½ tsp turmeric

1–2 cinnamon sticks

½–1 butternut squash, about 450 g/1 lb, peeled, deseeded and cut into small chunks

225 g/8 oz sweet potatoes, cut into small chunks

85 g/3 oz ready-to-eat prunes

450–600 ml/16 fl oz–1 pint vegetable stock

4 tomatoes, chopped

400 g/14 oz canned chickpeas, drained and rinsed

1 tbsp chopped fresh coriander, to garnish

Method

1. Heat the oil in a large heavy-based saucepan with a tight-fitting lid and cook the onion, garlic, chilli and aubergine, stirring frequently, for 5–8 minutes, until softened.

2. Add the ginger, cumin, ground coriander and saffron and cook, stirring constantly, for 2 minutes. Bruise the cinnamon stick.

3. Add the cinnamon, squash, sweet potatoes, prunes, stock and tomatoes to the saucepan and bring to the boil. Reduce the heat, cover and simmer, stirring occasionally, for 20 minutes. Add the chickpeas to the saucepan and cook for a further 10 minutes. Discard the cinnamon stick and serve garnished with the fresh coriander.

BEANS

HAM & BLACK-EYED BEAN STEW

Serves: 4 **Prep: 25 mins** **Cook: 1¾ hours–1 hour 50 mins**

Ingredients

- 450–550 g/1–1 lb 4 oz lean gammon
- 2½ tbsp olive oil
- 1 onion, chopped
- 2–3 garlic cloves, chopped
- 2 celery sticks, chopped
- 175 g/6 oz carrots, sliced
- 1 cinnamon stick, bruised
- ½ tsp ground cloves
- ¼ tsp freshly grated nutmeg
- 1 tsp dried oregano
- 450 ml/16 fl oz chicken stock or vegetable stock
- 1–2 tbsp maple syrup
- 3 large spicy sausages, or about 225 g/8 oz chorizo
- 400 g/14 oz canned black-eyed beans, drained and rinsed
- 1 orange pepper, deseeded and chopped
- 1 tbsp cornflour
- 2 tbsp water
- pepper (optional)

Method

1. Trim off any fat or skin from the gammon and cut into 4-cm/1½-inch chunks. Heat 1 tablespoon of the oil in a heavy-based saucepan or flameproof casserole and cook the gammon over a high heat, stirring frequently, for 5 minutes, or until brown. Using a slotted spoon, remove from the saucepan and set aside.

2. Add the onion, garlic, celery and carrots to the saucepan with 1 tablespoon of the remaining oil and cook over a medium heat, stirring frequently, for 5 minutes, or until softened. Add the cinnamon, cloves and nutmeg, season to taste with pepper, if using, and cook, stirring constantly, for 2 minutes.

3. Return the gammon to the saucepan.

4. Add the oregano, stock and maple syrup to taste, then bring to the boil, stirring. Cover and simmer, stirring occasionally, for 1 hour.

5. Heat the remaining oil in a frying pan and cook the sausages, turning frequently, until browned all over. Remove and cut each into 3–4 chunks, then add to the saucepan. Add the beans and orange pepper and simmer for a further 20 minutes. Blend the cornflour with the water and stir into the stew, then cook for 3–5 minutes. Remove the cinnamon stick and serve.

BEANS

VEGETABLE & LENTIL CASSEROLE

Serves: 4 **Prep:** 20–25 mins **Cook:** 2 hours

Ingredients

- 10 cloves
- 1 onion, peeled but kept whole
- 225 g/8 oz Puy or green lentils
- 1 bay leaf
- 1.5 litres/2¾ pints vegetable stock
- 2 leeks, sliced
- 2 potatoes, diced
- 2 carrots, chopped
- 3 courgettes, sliced
- 1 celery stick, chopped
- 1 red pepper, deseeded and chopped
- 1 tbsp lemon juice
- salt and pepper (optional)

Method

1. Preheat the oven to 180°C/350°F/Gas Mark 4.
2. Press the cloves into the onion. Put the lentils into a large casserole, add the onion and bay leaf and pour in the stock. Cover and cook in the preheated oven for 1 hour.
3. Remove the onion and discard the cloves. Slice the onion and return it to the casserole with all the vegetables. Stir thoroughly and season to taste with salt and pepper, if using. Cover and return to the oven for 1 hour.
4. Discard the bay leaf. Stir in the lemon juice and serve immediately.

BEANS

BEAN & TOMATO CASSEROLE WITH PARMESAN TOASTS

Serves: 4 **Prep: 20 mins** **Cook: 35 mins**

Ingredients

1 large onion

15–20 fresh sage leaves

4 tbsp extra virgin olive oil, plus extra for drizzling

25 g/1 oz butter

2 large garlic cloves, sliced

1 tbsp tomato purée and 800 g/1 lb 12 oz canned chopped tomatoes

350 g/12 oz canned borlotti beans, drained and rinsed

300 ml/10 fl oz stock

4 tbsp chopped fresh flat-leaf parsley

50 g/1¾ oz grated Parmesan cheese

8 thin slices ciabatta

salt and pepper (optional)

fresh sage sprigs, to garnish

Method

1. Thinly slice the onion and slice the sage leaves. Heat the oil and butter in a large saucepan over a medium heat. Add the onion and sage and fry for 5 minutes, until the onion is translucent. Add the garlic and fry for 2 minutes, until just coloured. Add the tomato purée and fry for 1 minute, stirring.

2. Stir in the tomatoes, beans and stock and season with salt and pepper, if using. Bring to the boil, then reduce the heat and simmer, partially covered, for 20 minutes. Add the parsley and half the cheese.

3. Ladle the beans into warmed bowls. Top each plate with 2 slices of ciabatta. Drizzle the bread with oil and sprinkle over the remaining cheese. Garnish with sage sprigs and serve immediately.

BEANS

VEGETABLE & PUY GOULASH

Serves: 4 **Prep: 25 mins** plus soaking **Cook: 1 hour–1 hour 5 mins**

Ingredients

- 15 g/½ oz sun-dried tomatoes (not in oil), chopped
- 225 g/8 oz Puy lentils
- 600 ml/1 pint water
- 2 tbsp olive oil
- ½–1 tsp crushed dried chillies
- 2–3 garlic cloves, chopped
- 1 large onion, cut into small wedges
- 1 small celeriac, cut into small chunks
- 225 g/8 oz carrots, sliced
- 225 g/8 oz new potatoes, scrubbed and cut into chunks
- 1 small acorn squash, deseeded, peeled and cut into small chunks, about 225 g/8 oz prepared weight
- 2 tbsp tomato purée
- 300 ml/10 fl oz vegetable stock
- 1–2 tsp hot paprika
- a few fresh thyme sprigs, plus extra to garnish
- 450 g/1 lb ripe tomatoes
- soured cream and crusty bread, to serve

Method

1. Put the sun-dried tomatoes in a small heatproof bowl, cover with almost-boiling water and leave to soak for 15–20 minutes. Drain, reserving the soaking liquid.

2. Meanwhile, rinse and drain the lentils, then put them in a saucepan with the water and bring to the boil. Reduce the heat, cover and simmer for 15 minutes. Drain and set aside.

3. Heat the oil in a large heavy-based saucepan with a tight-fitting lid and cook the chillies, garlic and vegetables, stirring frequently, for 5–8 minutes, until softened. Blend the tomato purée with a little of the stock in a jug and pour over the vegetable mixture, then add the remaining stock, the lentils, the sun-dried tomatoes and their soaking liquid, and the paprika and thyme sprigs.

4. Bring to the boil, then reduce the heat, cover and simmer for 15 minutes. Add the fresh tomatoes and simmer for a further 15 minutes, or until the vegetables and lentils are tender. Transfer to warmed serving bowls, top with spoonfuls of soured cream and garnish with thyme sprigs. Serve immediately with crusty bread.

BEANS

LENTIL BOLOGNAISE

Serves: 4 **Prep: 20 mins** **Cook: 20–25 mins**

Ingredients

- 25 g/1 oz onion
- 25 g/1 oz leek
- 25 g/1 oz celery
- 25 g/1 oz carrot
- 25 g/1 oz courgette
- 25 g/1 oz green pepper
- 85 g/3 oz flat mushrooms
- 1 tsp vegetable oil
- 1 tsp crushed garlic
- 4 tbsp red wine
- pinch of dried thyme
- 400 g/14 oz canned chopped tomatoes, strained, with juice and pulp reserved separately
- 4 tbsp dried Puy or green lentils, cooked
- 2 tsp lemon juice
- 1 tsp sugar
- 3 tbsp chopped fresh basil, plus extra to garnish
- salt and pepper (optional)
- cooked spaghetti, to serve

Method

1. Finely chop the onion, leek, celery, carrot and courgette. Deseed and finely chop the green pepper and dice the mushrooms.

2. Place a large saucepan over a low heat, add the oil and garlic and cook, stirring, until golden brown. Add all the vegetables, except the mushrooms, increase the heat to medium and cook, stirring occasionally, for 10–12 minutes, or until softened and there is no liquid from the vegetables left in the pan.

3. Add the mushrooms and increase the heat to high. Add the wine and cook for 2 minutes, then stir in the thyme and the juice from the tomatoes and cook until reduced by half.

4. Add the lentils, stir in the tomato pulp and cook for a further 3–4 minutes. Remove the pan from the heat and stir in the lemon juice, sugar and basil. Season to taste with salt and pepper, if using.

5. Garnish with basil and serve the sauce immediately with spaghetti.

BEANS

SPICY AUBERGINE & CHICKPEA CASSEROLE

Serves: 4–6 **Prep: 25 mins** **Cook: 55 mins**

Ingredients

4 tbsp olive oil

1 large onion, chopped

1 tbsp cumin seeds, crushed

½ tsp allspice berries, crushed

½ tsp salt

¼ tsp pepper

2 garlic cloves, thinly sliced

1 large red pepper, deseeded and cut into 2.5-cm/1-inch pieces

2 aubergines, thickly sliced and cut into segments

800 g/1 lb 12 oz canned chickpeas, drained and rinsed

400 g/14 oz canned chopped tomatoes

500 ml/18 fl oz vegetable stock

½ head of cabbage, tough stalks removed, about 280 g/10 oz in total

salt and pepper (optional)

Method

1. Heat the oil in a 4-litre/7-pint flameproof casserole. Add the onion, cumin, allspice, ½ teaspoon salt and ¼ teaspoon pepper. Fry over a medium-high heat for 5 minutes, until the onion is soft but not coloured.

2. Add the garlic, red pepper and aubergines and fry for a further 5 minutes, until the red pepper and aubergines are beginning to soften.

3. Stir in the chickpeas, tomatoes and stock. Bring to the boil, then reduce the heat and simmer, covered, for 30 minutes.

4. Meanwhile, slice the cabbage leaves into ribbons. Add the cabbage to the casserole, cover and simmer for 10–12 minutes, until the cabbage is tender but still bright green. Taste and adjust the seasoning, adding salt and pepper if using. Serve immediately.

BEANS

INDEX

apples
- Chicken & Apple Pot 34
- Sweet Potato & Apple Soup 158

apricots
- Lamb Pilaf 94
- Mediterranean Lamb with Apricots & Pistachios 82
- Moroccan-Style Turkey 54
- Tagine of Lamb 80

asparagus: Brown Rice Risotto Primavera 162

aubergines
- Aubergine Gratin 197
- Moroccan Vegetable & Chickpea Stew 242
- Ratatouille Sausage Bake 88
- Spanish Vegetable Stew 170
- Spicy Aubergine & Chickpea Casserole 252
- Spicy Vegetable Stew 190
- Tagine of Lamb 80
- Tuscan Bean Stew 224
- Warm Vegetable Medley 160

barley
- Chicken & Barley Stew 50
- Chorizo with Barley & Butter Beans 96
- Turkey & Barley Stew 28

beans
- Bean & Tomato Casserole with Parmesan Toasts 247
- Beef in Black Bean Sauce 81
- Cauliflower & Butter Bean Stew 220
- Chicken, Squash & Bean Casserole 234
- Chilli Bean Stew 229
- Chilli Con Carne 86
- Chorizo with Barley & Butter Beans 96
- Country-Style Ham with Pinto Beans 90
- Ham & Black-Eyed Bean Stew 244
- Haricot Beans & Vegetable Casserole 232
- Italian Turkey Stew 40
- Jerk Turkey & Black-Eyed Bean Soup 230
- Kidney Bean, Pumpkin & Tomato Stew 210
- Mexican Beef & Bean Bowl 214
- Mexican Black Bean Pan-Fry 208
- Mexican Quinoa Chilli 166
- Minestrone Soup 164
- Prawn & Fermented Black Bean Soup 219
- Pumpkin & Haricot Bean Soup 218
- Red Kidney Bean Curry 216
- Ribollita 238
- Sausage & Bean Casserole 98
- Spanish Vegetable Stew 170
- Spiced Chicken Stew 48
- Spicy Bean Chilli 231
- Spicy Vegetable Stew 190
- Tuna Chowder 148
- Tuscan Bean Stew 224

beef
- Beef & Vegetable Stew with Corn 100
- Beef in Beer with Herbed Dumplings 92
- Beef in Black Bean Sauce 81
- Beer-Braised Beef Short Ribs 62
- Chilli Con Carne 86
- Chunky Potato & Beef Soup 78
- Hearty Beet Stew 70
- Large Mixed Grill 64
- Mexican Beef & Bean Bowl 214
- Mexican Quinoa Chilli 166
- One Pot Lasagne 76
- Texas Lone-Star Chilli 102

broad beans
- Chilli Bean Stew 229
- Pesto Potatoes & Beans 182
- Pork with Mixed Green Beans 97
- Squid & Prawn Stew 130

broccoli
- Lentil & Rice Casserole 236
- Lentil Quinoa Pot 212

cabbage
- Cabbage & Walnut Stir-Fry 180
- Minestrone Soup 164
- Ribollita 238
- Spicy Aubergine & Chickpea Casserole 252

cauliflower
- Cauliflower & Butter Bean Stew 220
- Cauliflower & Sweet Potato Curry 192
- Cauliflower Dhal Soup 228
- Turkey & Lentil Soup 14

celeriac
- Celeriac & New Potato Smash 179
- Vegetable & Puy Goulash 248

chicken
- Baked Chicken & Chorizo Paella 24
- Chicken & Apple Pot 34
- Chicken & Barley Stew 50
- Chicken & Lentil Soup 19
- Chicken & Pumpkin Casserole 36
- Chicken & Sweet Potato Bake 32
- Chicken Cacciatore 29
- Chicken with 40 Garlic Cloves 22
- Chicken with Goat's Cheese & Mushroom Sauce 31
- Chicken Noodle Soup 12
- Chicken Soup with Leeks & Rice 18
- Chicken, Squash & Bean Casserole 234
- Coq au Vin 47
- Cream of Chicken Soup 26
- Hunter's Chicken 46
- Mexican Chicken, Chilli & Potato Pot 44
- Prawn & Chicken Paella 126
- Roast Chicken 52
- Roast Chicken Wings with Garlic 10
- Saffron, Chicken & Vegetable Stew 20
- Spiced Chicken Stew 48

chickpeas
- Chilli Bean Stew 229
- Moroccan-Style Turkey 54
- Moroccan Vegetable & Chickpea Stew 242
- Spicy Chickpea & Chickpea Casserole 252
- Spicy Chickpea & Red Pepper Soup 222
- Squash, Kale & Farro Stew 204
- Sweet Potato & Chickpea Curry 210
- Vegetable Stew with Couscous 174

chorizo
- Baked Chicken & Chorizo Paella 24
- Chicken & Pumpkin Casserole 36
- Chorizo & Blue Cheese Omelette 68
- Chorizo with Barley & Butter Beans 96
- Duck Jambalaya Stew 42
- Large Mixed Grill 64
- Prawn & Chicken Paella 126

cod
- Fish Stew with Cider 140
- Goan-Style Seafood Curry 120
- Spiced Baked Cod with Harissa & Pine Nut Crust 138

courgettes
- Brown Rice Risotto Primavera 162
- One Pot Lasagne 76
- Ratatouille Sausage Bake 88
- Spanish Vegetable Stew 170
- Vegetable & Lentil Casserole 246

duck
- Duck Jambalaya Stew 42
- Duck Legs with Olives 16
- Roasted Duck Soup with Mushrooms & Eggs 8

eggs
- Chorizo & Blue Cheese Omelette 68
- Egg-Fried Rice with Vegetables 184
- Large Mixed Grill 64
- Persian Herb Frittata 200
- Roasted Duck Soup with Mushrooms & Eggs 8
- Shakshouka 194

fennel
- Bouillabaisse 134
- Saffron & Prawn Broth 112
- Tuscan Bean Stew 224
- Vegetable Pho 198

fish & seafood
- Baked Sea Bass 122
- Bouillabaisse 134
- Coconut Fish Curry 129
- Crab & Vegetable Soup 116
- Mediterranean Fish Casserole 147
- Miso Fish Soup 119
- One-Pot Clam Bake 154
- Seven Seas Soup 132
- see also cod; haddock; monkfish; mussels; prawns; salmon; squid; swordfish; tuna

french beans
- Chicken Noodle Soup 12
- Lentil & Rice Casserole 236
- Pork with Mixed Green Beans 97
- Vegetable Stew with Couscous 174

haddock
- Minted Potato & Haddock One Pot 108
- Mixed Seafood Chowder 114
- Seafood Gumbo 150

ham & gammon
- Country-Style Ham with Pinto Beans 90
- Duck Jambalaya Stew 42
- Ham & Black-Eyed Bean Stew 244
- Ham & Lentil Soup 79
- Large Mixed Grill 64
- Minestrone Soup 164
- Split Pea & Ham Soup 226

kale
- Kale, Sweet Potato & Peanut Stew 188
- Squash, Kale & Farro Stew 204

lamb
- Cinnamon Lamb Casserole 104
- Kashmiri Lamb & Fennel Stew 84
- Lamb Pilaf 94
- Large Mixed Grill 64
- Mediterranean Lamb with Apricots & Pistachios 82
- Spring Lamb Stew 60
- Tagine of Lamb 80

lentils
- Butternut Squash & Lentil Stew 168
- Cauliflower Dhal Soup 228
- Chicken & Lentil Soup 19
- Ham & Lentil Soup 79
- Lentil & Rice Casserole 236
- Lentil Bolognaise 250
- Lentil Quinoa Pot 212
- Turkey & Lentil Soup 14
- Vegetable & Puy Goulash 248

monkfish
- Fish Stew with Cider 140
- Goan-Style Seafood Curry 120
- Monkfish Ragoût 152
- Seafood Gumbo 150

mushrooms
- Chicken with Goat's Cheese & Mushroom Sauce 31

Ginger Pork with Shiitake Mushrooms 58
Potato & Mushroom Pie 176
Roasted Duck Soup with Mushrooms & Eggs 8
Tandoori Mushroom Curry 172
Tuna Noodle Casserole 136
Turkey Stroganoff 38
Vegetable Pho 198

mussels
Bouillabaisse 134
Mixed Seafood Chowder 114
Moules Marinière 131
Mussels in Cider 128
Prawn & Chicken Paella 126

noodles
Chicken Noodle Soup 12
Hot & Sour Noodles with Tofu 202
Miso Fish Soup 119
Roasted Duck Soup with Mushrooms & Eggs 8
Salmon & Udon Broth 118
Tuna Noodle casserole 136
Udon Noodle Stir-Fry with Fish Cake & Ginger 124
Vegetable Pho 198

nuts
Cabbage & Walnut Stir-Fry 180
Chestnut & Pancetta Soup 69
Kale, Sweet Potato & Peanut Stew 188
Mediterranean Lamb with Apricots & Pistachios 82
Persian Herb Frittata 200
Pork with Mixed Green Beans 97
Pork Stir-Fry with Cashews, Lime, & Mint 72
Sweet Potato & Chickpea Curry 210
Yogurt, Pomegranate & Peanut Raita 169

parsnips: Onion & Root Vegetable Winter Roast 186

pasta
Creamy Prawn Pasta 110
Minestrone Soup 164

peas
Baked Chicken & Chorizo Paella 24
Braised Peas with Lettuce & Tarragon 196
Cauliflower & Sweet Potato Curry 192
Potato & Haddock One Pot 108
Prawn & Chicken Paella 126
Spring Lamb Stew 60
Tandoori Mushroom Curry 172

peppers
Beef in Black Bean Sauce 81
Chicken & Sweet Potato Bake 32
Chorizo with Barley & Butter Beans 96
Country-Style Ham with Pinto Beans 90

Crab & Vegetable Soup 116
Italian Turkey Stew 40
Mexican Beef & Bean Bowl 214
Minestrone Soup 164
Ratatouille Sausage Bake 88
Sausage & Bean Casserole 98
Seafood Gumbo 150
Shakshouka 194
Spiced Chicken Stew 48
Spicy Chickpea & Red Pepper Soup 222
Spicy Vegetable Stew 190

pomegranates
Lentil Quinoa Pot 212
Yogurt, Pomegranate & Peanut Raita 169

pork
Ginger Pork with Shiitake Mushrooms 58
Pork Hot Pot 74
Pork Medallions in a Creamy Sauce 66
Pork Stir-Fry with Cashews, Lime & Mint 72
Pork with Mixed Green Beans 97

potatoes
Celeriac & New Potato Smash 199
Chunky Potato & Beef Soup 78
Minted Potato & Haddock One Pot 108
Pesto Potatoes & Beans 182
Potato & Lemon Casserole 181
Potato & Mushroom Pie 176
Salmon & Potato Casserole 144

prawns
Baked Chicken & Chorizo Paella 24
Bouillabaisse 134
Creamy Prawn Pasta 110
Goan-Style Seafood Curry 120
One-Pot Clam Bake 154
Prawn & Chicken Paella 126
Prawn & Fermented Black Bean Soup 219
Prawns in Mediterranean Sauce 142
Saffron & Prawn Broth 112
Seafood Gumbo 150
Squid & Prawn Stew 130
Udon Noodle Stir-Fry with Fish Cake & Ginger 124

pumpkin & squash
Butternut Squash & Lentil Stew 168
Chicken & Pumpkin Casserole 36
Chicken, Squash & Bean Casserole 234
Kidney Bean, Pumpkin & Tomato Stew 240
Moroccan Vegetable & Chickpea Stew 242
Pumpkin & Haricot Bean Soup 218
Squash, Kale & Farro Stew 204
Vegetable & Puy Goulash 248

quinoa
Lentil Quinoa Pot 212
Mexican Quinoa Chilli 166

rice
Baked Chicken & Chorizo Paella 24
Brown Rice Risotto Primavera 162
Chicken Soup with Leeks & Rice 18
Egg-Fried Rice with Vegetables 184
Lamb Pilaf 94
Lentil & Rice Casserole 236
Prawn & Chicken Paella 126

salmon
Mixed Seafood Chowder 114
Salmon & Potato Casserole 144
Salmon & Udon Broth 118

sausages
Ham & Black-Eyed Bean Stew 244
Large Mixed Grill 64
One-Pot Clam Bake 154
Ratatouille Sausage Bake 88
Sausage & Bean Casserole 98
see also chorizo

soya beans
Lentil Quinoa Pot 212
Prawn & Fermented Black Bean Soup 219

spinach
Spicy Chickpea & Red Pepper Soup 222
Sweet Potato & Chickpea Curry 210
Vegetable Stew with Couscous 174

squid
Squid & Prawn Stew 130

sweet potatoes
Cauliflower & Sweet Potato Curry 192
Chicken & Sweet Potato Bake 32
Kale, Sweet Potato & Peanut Stew 188
Mexican Chicken, Chilli & Potato Pot 44
Moroccan Vegetable & Chickpea Stew 242
Onion & Root Vegetable Winter Roast 186
Sweet Potato & Apple Soup 158
Sweet Potato & Chickpea Curry 210

sweetcorn
Beef & Vegetable Stew with Corn 100
Chunky Potato & Beef Soup 78
Crab & Vegetable Soup 116
Egg-Fried Rice with Vegetables 184
Lentil & Rice Casserole 236
Mexican Black Bean Pan-Fry 208
One-Pot Clam Bake 154
Prawn & Fermented Black Bean Soup 219
Spiced Chicken Stew 48

swordfish
Mediterranean Swordfish 146
Swordfish with Tomatoes & Olives 132

tofu
Hot & Sour Noodles with Tofu 202
Tofu Parcels 178

tomatoes
Aubergine Gratin 197
Bean & Tomato Casserole 247
Bouillabaisse 134
Chicken & Pumpkin Casserole 36
Chicken Cacciatore 29
Chilli Con Carne 86
Duck Jambalaya Stew 42
Duck Legs with Olives 16
Haricot Beans & Vegetable Casserole 232
Hunter's Chicken 46
Jerk Turkey & Black-Eyed Bean Soup 230
Kidney Bean, Pumpkin & Tomato Stew 240
Lentil & Rice Casserole 236
Mediterranean Swordfish 146
Mexican Black Bean Pan-Fry 208
Mexican Quinoa Chilli 166
Minestrone Soup 164
Monkfish Ragoût 152
One Pot Lasagne 76
Pork Hot Pot 74
Ribollita 238
Sausage & Bean Casserole 98
Shakshouka 194
Spanish Vegetable Stew 170
Spiced Chicken Stew 48
Spicy Bean Chilli 231
Spicy Vegetable Stew 190
Swordfish with Tomatoes & Olives 132
Tandoori Mushroom Curry 172
Texas Lone-Star Chilli 102
Tuscan Bean Stew 224
Vegetable & Puy Goulash 248
Vegetable Stew with Couscous 174

tuna
Tuna Chowder 148
Tuna Noodle Casserole 136

turkey
Italian Turkey Stew 40
Jerk Turkey & Black-Eyed Bean Soup 230
Mexican Black Bean Pan-Fry 208
Moroccan-Style Turkey 54
Stir-Fried Turkey with Cranberry Glaze 30
Turkey & Barley Stew 28
Turkey & Lentil Soup 14
Turkey Stroganoff 38

turnips
Potato & Lemon Casserole 181
Spring Lamb Stew 60

INDEX

This edition published by Parragon Books Ltd in 2016
LOVE FOOD is an imprint of Parragon Books Ltd

Parragon Books Ltd
Chartist House
15–17 Trim Street
Bath BA1 1HA, UK
www.parragon.com/lovefood

Copyright © Parragon Books Ltd 2016

LOVE FOOD and the accompanying heart device is a registered trademark of Parragon Books Ltd in Australia, the UK, USA, India and the EU.

All rights reserved. No part of this publication may be reproduced, stored in a retrieval system or transmitted, in any form or by any means, electronic, mechanical, photocopying, recording or otherwise, without the prior permission of the copyright holder.

ISBN 978-1-4748-4147-4

Printed in China

Introduction by Anne Sheasby
Cover photography by Ian Garlick

The cover shot shows the Chicken & Pumpkin Casserole on page 36.

Notes for the Reader
This book uses both metric and imperial measurements. Follow the same units of measurement throughout; do not mix metric and imperial. All spoon measurements are level: teaspoons are assumed to be 5 ml, and tablespoons are assumed to be 15 ml. Unless otherwise stated, milk is assumed to be full fat, eggs and individual fruits and vegetables are medium, pepper is freshly ground black pepper and salt is table salt. A pinch of salt is calculated as $1/16$ of a teaspoon. Unless otherwise stated, all root vegetables should be peeled prior to using.

The times given are an approximate guide only. Preparation times differ according to the techniques used by different people and the cooking times may also vary from those given.

For best results, use a food thermometer when cooking meat. Check the latest government guidelines for current advice.

150 Recipes series